AngularJS

Brad Green and Shyam Seshadri

O'REILLY®

Beijing · Cambridge · Farnham · Köln · Sebastopol · Tokyo

AngularJS

by Brad Green and Shyam Seshadri

Printed in the United States of America.

Published by O'Reilly Media, Inc., 1005 Gravenstein Highway North, Sebastopol, CA 95472.

O'Reilly books may be purchased for educational, business, or sales promotional use. Online editions are also available for most titles (*http://my.safaribooksonline.com*). For more information, contact our corporate/institutional sales department: 800-998-9938 or *corporate@oreilly.com*.

Editors: Simon St. Laurent and Meghan Blanchette	**Indexer:** Judith McConville
Production Editor: Melanie Yarbrough	**Cover Designer:** Randy Comer
Copyeditor: Rachel Leach	**Interior Designer:** David Futato
Proofreader: Jilly Gagnon	**Illustrator:** Rebecca Demarest

April 2013: First Edition

Revision History for the First Edition:

2013-04-05: First release

See *http://oreilly.com/catalog/errata.csp?isbn=9781449344856* for release details.

ISBN: 978-1-449-34485-6

LSI

Table of Contents

Preface

I can trace Angular's beginnings to 2009, on a project called Google Feedback. We'd gone through months of frustration with our development speed and ability to write testable code. At around the six month mark, we had around 17,000 lines of front-end code. At that point, one of the team members, Misko Hevery, made a bold statement that he'd be able to rewrite the whole thing in two weeks using an open source library that he'd created as a hobby.

I figured that a two week delay couldn't hurt us that much and we'd at least be entertained by Misko scrambling to build something. Misko missed his time estimate. It took three weeks. We were all astounded, but even more astounding was that the line count for this new app had dropped from 17,000 to a mere 1,500. It seemed that Misko was onto something worth pursuing.

Misko and I decided we'd built a team around the concepts he started with a simple charter: to simplify the web developer's experience. Shyam Seshadri, this book's co-author, went on to lead the Google Feedback team in developing Angular's first shipping application.

Since then, we've developed Angular with guidance both from teams at Google and from hundreds of open source contributors around the world. Thousands of developers rely on Angular in their daily work and contribute to an amazing support network.

We're excited to learn what you'll teach us.

Conventions Used in This Book

The following typographical conventions are used in this book:

Italic
>   Indicates new terms, URLs, email addresses, filenames, and file extensions.

`Constant width`

Used for program listings, as well as within paragraphs to refer to program elements such as variable or function names, databases, data types, environment variables, statements, and keywords.

`Constant width bold`

Shows commands or other text that should be typed literally by the user.

`Constant width italic`

Shows text that should be replaced with user-supplied values or by values determined by context.

 This icon signifies a tip, suggestion, or general note.

 This icon indicates a warning or caution.

Using Code Examples

This book is here to help you get your job done. In general, if this book includes code examples, you may use the code in this book in your programs and documentation. You do not need to contact us for permission unless you're reproducing a significant portion of the code. For example, writing a program that uses several chunks of code from this book does not require permission. Selling or distributing a CD-ROM of examples from O'Reilly books does require permission. Answering a question by citing this book and quoting example code does not require permission. Incorporating a significant amount of example code from this book into your product's documentation does require permission.

We appreciate, but do not require, attribution. An attribution usually includes the title, author, publisher, and ISBN. For example: "*AngularJS* by Brad Green and Shyam Seshadri (O'Reilly). Copyright 2013 Brad Green and Shyam Seshadri, 978-1-449-34485-6."

If you feel your use of code examples falls outside fair use or the permission given above, feel free to contact us at *permissions@oreilly.com*.

Safari® Books Online

 *Safari Books Online* is an on-demand digital library that delivers expert content in both book and video form from the world's leading authors in technology and business.

Technology professionals, software developers, web designers, and business and creative professionals use Safari Books Online as their primary resource for research, problem solving, learning, and certification training.

Safari Books Online offers a range of product mixes and pricing programs for organizations, government agencies, and individuals. Subscribers have access to thousands of books, training videos, and prepublication manuscripts in one fully searchable database from publishers like O'Reilly Media, Prentice Hall Professional, Addison-Wesley Professional, Microsoft Press, Sams, Que, Peachpit Press, Focal Press, Cisco Press, John Wiley & Sons, Syngress, Morgan Kaufmann, IBM Redbooks, Packt, Adobe Press, FT Press, Apress, Manning, New Riders, McGraw-Hill, Jones & Bartlett, Course Technology, and dozens more. For more information about Safari Books Online, please visit us online.

How to Contact Us

Please address comments and questions concerning this book to the publisher:

O'Reilly Media, Inc.
1005 Gravenstein Highway North
Sebastopol, CA 95472
800-998-9938 (in the United States or Canada)
707-829-0515 (international or local)
707-829-0104 (fax)

We have a web page for this book, where we list errata, examples, and any additional information. You can access this page at *http://oreil.ly/angularJS*.

To comment or ask technical questions about this book, send email to *bookquestions@oreilly.com*.

For more information about our books, courses, conferences, and news, see our website at *http://www.oreilly.com*.

Find us on Facebook: *http://facebook.com/oreilly*

Follow us on Twitter: *http://twitter.com/oreillymedia*

Watch us on YouTube: *http://www.youtube.com/oreillymedia*

Acknowledgments

We'd like to give special thanks to Misko Hevery, father of Angular, for having the courage to think very differently about how we write web applications and to drive it into reality; to Igor Minar for bringing stability and structure to the Angular project and for building the roots of today's awesome open source community; to Vojta Jina for creating many parts of Angular, and for giving us the fastest test runner the world has ever seen; to Naomi Black, John Lindquist, and Mathias Matias Niemelä for their expert editing assistance. And finally, thank you to the Angular community for their contributions, and for teaching us about making Angular great through feedback from building real applications.

CHAPTER 1

Introduction to AngularJS

Our ability to create amazing web-based apps is incredible, but the complexity involved in making these apps is similarly incredible. We on the Angular team wanted to relieve the pain involved with developing AJAX applications. At Google, we'd worked through the hard lessons of building large web applications like Gmail, Maps, Calendar, and several others. We thought we might be able to use these experiences to benefit everyone.

We wanted writing web apps to feel more like the first time we wrote a few lines of code and stood back in amazement at what we'd made happen. We wanted the coding process to feel more like creating and less like trying to satisfy the strange inner workings of web browsers.

At the same time, we wanted an environment that helped us make the design choices that make apps easy to create and understand from the start, but that continue to be the right choices to make our apps easy to test, extend, and maintain as they grow large.

We've tried to do this in the Angular framework. We're very excited about the results we've achieved. A lot of credit goes to the open source community around Angular who do a fantastic job supporting each other and who have taught us many things. We hope you'll join our community and help us learn how Angular can be even better.

Some of the larger and more involved examples and code snippets are available on a GitHub repository for you to look at, fork, and play with at our GitHub page (*http://github.com/shyamseshadri/angularjs-book*).

Concepts

There are a few core ideas that you'll use throughout an Angular app. As it turns out, we didn't invent any of these. Instead, we've borrowed heavily from successful idioms in other development environments and implemented them in a way that embraces HTML, browsers, and many other familiar web standards.

Client-Side Templates

Multi-page web applications create their HTML by assembling and joining it with data on the server, and then shipping the finished pages up to the browser. Most single-page applications—also known as AJAX apps—do this as well, to some extent. Angular is different in that the template and data get shipped to the browser to be assembled there. The role of the server then becomes only to serve as static resources for the templates and to properly serve the data required by those templates.

Let's see an example of what assembling this data and template on the browser looks like in Angular. We'll take the obligatory Hello, World example, but instead of writing "Hello, World" as a single string, let's structure the greeting "Hello" as data that we could change later.

For it, we'll create our template in *hello.html*:

```
<html ng-app>
<head>
  <script src="angular.js"></script>
  <script src="controllers.js"></script>
</head>
<body>
  <div ng-controller='HelloController'>
    <p>{{greeting.text}}, World</p>
  </div>
</body>
</html>
```

And our logic in *controllers.js*:

```
function HelloController($scope) {
  $scope.greeting = { text: 'Hello' };
}
```

Loading *hello.html* into any browser will then produce what we see in Figure 1-1:

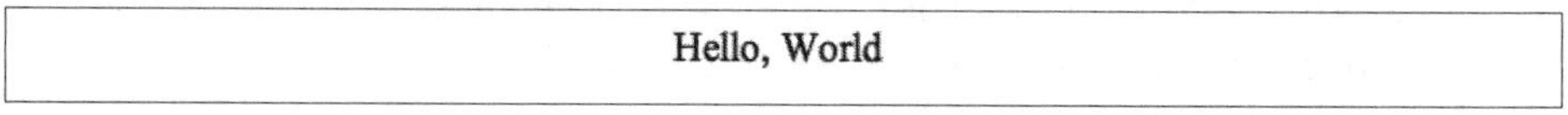

Hello, World

Figure 1-1. Hello, World

There are a few interesting things to note here in comparison with most methods in widespread use today:

- There are no classes or IDs in the HTML to identify where to attach event listeners.

- When HelloController set the greeting.text to *Hello*, we didn't have to register any event listeners or write any callbacks.

- `HelloController` is a plain JavaScript class, and doesn't inherit from anything that Angular provides.

- `HelloController` got the `$scope` object that it needed without having to create it.

- We didn't have to call the `HelloController`'s constructor ourselves, or figure out when to call it.

We'll look at more differences soon, but it should be clear already that Angular applications are structured very differently than similar applications were in the past.

Why have we made these design choices and how does Angular work? Let's look at some good ideas Angular stole from elsewhere.

Model View Controller (MVC)

MVC application structure was introduced in the 1970s as part of Smalltalk. From its start in Smalltalk, MVC became popular in nearly every desktop development environment where user interfaces were involved. Whether you were using C++, Java, or Objective-C, there was some flavor of MVC available. Until recently, however, MVC was all but foreign to web development.

The core idea behind MVC is that you have clear separation in your code between managing its data (model), the application logic (controller), and presenting the data to the user (view).

The view gets data from the model to display to the user. When a user interacts with the application by clicking or typing, the controller responds by changing data in the model. Finally, the model notifies the view that a change has occurred so that it can update what it displays.

In Angular applications, the view is the Document Object Model (DOM), the controllers are JavaScript classes, and the model data is stored in object properties.

We think MVC is neat for several reasons. First, it gives you a mental model for where to put what, so you don't have to invent it every time. Other folks collaborating on your project will have an instant leg up on understanding what you've written, as they'll know you're using MVC structure to organize your code. Perhaps most importantly, we'll claim that it delivers great benefits in making your app easier to extend, maintain, and test.

Data Binding

Before AJAX single-page apps were common, platforms like Rails, PHP, or JSP helped us create the user interface (UI) by merging strings of HTML with data before sending it to the users to display it.

Libraries like jQuery extended this model to the client and let us follow a similar style, but with the ability to update, part of the DOM separately, rather than updating the whole page. Here, we merge template HTML strings with data, then insert the result where we want it in the DOM by setting innerHtml on a placeholder element.

This all works pretty well, but when you want to insert fresher data into the UI, or change the data based on user input, you need to do quite a bit of non-trivial work to make sure you get the data into the correct state, both in the UI and in JavaScript properties.

But what if we could have all this work done for us without writing code? What if we could just declare which parts of the UI map to which JavaScript properties and have them sync automatically? This style of programming is called data binding. We included it in Angular because it works great with MVC to eliminate code when writing your view and model. Most of the work in moving data from one to the other just happens automatically.

To see this in action, let's take the first example and make it dynamic. As is, the Hello Controller sets the model greeting.text once and it never changes from then on. To make it *live*, let's change the example by adding a text input that can change the value of greeting.text as the user types.

Here's the new template:

```
<html ng-app>
<head>
  <script src="angular.js"></script>
  <script src="controllers.js"></script>
</head>
<body>
  <div ng-controller='HelloController'>
    <input ng-model='greeting.text'>
    <p>{{greeting.text}}, World</p>
  </div>
</body>
</html>
```

The controller, HelloController, can stay exactly the same.

Loading it in a browser, we'd see the screen captured in Figure 1-2.

Figure 1-2. The default state of the greeting app

If we replace *Hello* with *Hi* in the input field, we'd see the screen captured in Figure 1-3.

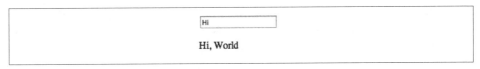

Figure 1-3. The Greeting App with input changed

Without ever registering a change listener on the input field, we have a UI that will dynamically update. The same would be true for changes coming to and from the server. In our controller, we could make a request to our server, get the response, and set `$scope.greeting.text` to equal what it returns. Angular would automatically update both the input and the text in the curly braces to that value.

Dependency Injection

We mentioned it before, but it bears repeating that there's a lot going on with `Hello Controller` that we didn't have to write. For example, the `$scope` object that does our data binding is passed to us automatically; we didn't have to create it by calling any function. We just *asked* for it by putting it in `HelloController`'s constructor.

As we'll find out in later chapters, `$scope` isn't the only thing we can ask for. If we want to data bind to the location URL in the user's browser, we can ask for an object that manages this by putting `$location` in our constructor, like so:

```
function HelloController($scope, $location) {
  $scope.greeting = { text: 'Hello' };
  // use $location for something good here...
}
```

We get this magical effect through Angular's dependency injection system. Dependency injection lets us follow a development style in which, instead of creating dependencies, our classes just ask for what they need.

This follows a design pattern called the Law of Demeter (*http://en.wikipedia.org/wiki/Law_of_Demeter*), also known as the principle of least knowledge. Since our `HelloController`'s job is to set up the initial state for the greeting model, this pattern would say that it shouldn't worry about anything else, like how `$scope` gets created, or where to find it.

This feature isn't just for objects created by the Angular framework. You can write the rest of this code as well.

Directives

One of the best parts of Angular is that you can write your templates as HTML. You can do this because at the core of the framework we've included a powerful DOM transformation engine that lets you extend HTML's syntax.

We've already seen several new attributes in our templates that aren't part of the HTML specification. Examples include the double-curly notation for data binding, ng-controller for specifying which controller oversees which part of the view, and ng-model, which binds an input to part of the model. We call these HTML extension directives.

Angular comes with many directives that help you define the view for your app. We'll see more of them soon. These directives can define what we commonly view as the template. They can declaratively set up how your application works or be used to create reusable components.

And you're not limited to the directives that Angular comes with. You can write your own to extend HTML's template abilities to do anything you can dream of.

An Example: Shopping Cart

Let's look at a slightly larger example that shows off a bit more of Angular. Let's imagine that we're going to build a shopping app. Somewhere in the app we'll need to show the user's shopping cart and let him edit it. Let's skip straight to that part.

```html
<html ng-app='myApp'>
<head>
  <title>Your Shopping Cart</title>
</head>
<body ng-controller='CartController'>
  <h1>Your Order</h1>
  <div ng-repeat='item in items'>
    <span>{{item.title}}</span>
    <input ng-model='item.quantity'>
    <span>{{item.price | currency}}</span>
    <span>{{item.price * item.quantity | currency}}</span>
    <button ng-click="remove($index)">Remove</button>
  </div>
  <script src="angular.js"></script>
  <script>
    function CartController($scope) {
      $scope.items = [
        {title: 'Paint pots', quantity: 8, price: 3.95},
        {title: 'Polka dots', quantity: 17, price: 12.95},
        {title: 'Pebbles', quantity: 5, price: 6.95}
      ];

      $scope.remove = function(index) {
        $scope.items.splice(index, 1);
      }
    }
  </script>
</body>
</html>
```

The resulting UI looks like the screenshot in Figure 1-4.

Your Shopping Cart

Pebbles [8] $3.95 $31.60 [Remove]
Paint pots [17] $12.95 $220.15 [Remove]
Prunes [5] $6.95 $34.75 [Remove]

Figure 1-4. The Shopping Cart UI

The following is a brief tour of what's going on here. The rest of the book is dedicated to a more in-depth explanation.

Let's start at the top:

```
<html ng-app>
```

The ng-app attribute tells Angular which parts of the page it should manage. Since we've placed it on the <html> element, we're telling Angular that we want it to manage the whole page. This will often be what you want, but you might want to place it on a <div> within the app if you're integrating Angular with an existing app that uses other methods to manage the page.

```
<body ng-controller='CartController'>
```

In Angular, you manage areas of the page with JavaScript classes called controllers. By including a controller in the body tag, I'm declaring that CartController will manage everything between <body> and </body>.

```
<div ng-repeat='item in items'>
```

The ng-repeat says to copy the DOM inside this <div> once for every element in an array called *items*. On every copy of the div, it will also set a property named *item* to the current element so we can use it in the template. As you can see, this results in three <div>s each, containing the product title, quantity, unit price, total price, and a button to remove the item entirely.

```
<span>{{item.title}}</span>
```

As we showed in the "Hello, World" example, data binding via {{ }} lets us insert the value of a variable into part of the page and keep it in sync. The full expression {{item.title}} retrieves the current item in the iteration and then inserts the contents of that item's title property into the DOM.

```
<input ng-model='item.quantity'>
```

The ng-model definition creates data binding between the input field and the value of item.quantity.

The {{ }} in the <span> sets up a one-way relationship that says "insert a value here." We want that effect, but the application also needs to know when the user changes the quantity so it can change the total price.

We'll keep changes in sync with our model by using ng-model. The ng-model declaration inserts the value of item.quantity into the text field, but it also automatically updates item.quantity whenever the user types a new value.

```
<span>{{item.price | currency}}</span>
<span>{{item.price * item.quantity | currency}}</span>
```

We want the unit price and total price to be formatted as dollars. Angular comes with a feature called filters that lets us transform text, and there's a bundled filter called currency that will do this dollar formatting for us. We'll look at filters more in the next chapter.

```
<button ng-click='remove($index)'>Remove</button>
```

This allows users to remove items from their carts by clicking a *Remove* button next to the product. We've set it up so that clicking this button calls a remove() function. We've also passed in $index, which contains the iteration number of the ng-repeat, so we know which item to remove.

```
function CartController($scope) {
```

This CartController manages the logic of the shopping cart. We'll tell Angular that the controller needs something called $scope by putting it here. The $scope is what lets us bind data to elements in the UI.

```
$scope.items = [
  {title: 'Paint pots', quantity: 8, price: 3.95},
  {title: 'Polka dots', quantity: 17, price: 12.95},
  {title: 'Pebbles', quantity: 5, price: 6.95}
];
```

By defining $scope.items, I've created a dummy data hash to represent the collection of items in the user's shopping cart. We want to make them available to data bind with the UI, so we'll add them to $scope.

Of course, a real version of this can't just work in memory, and will need to talk to a server to properly persist the data. We'll get to that in later chapters.

```
$scope.remove = function(index) {
  $scope.items.splice(index, 1);
}
```

We want the remove() function available to bind in the UI, so we've added this to $scope as well. For the in-memory version of the shopping cart, the remove() function can just delete items from the array. Because the list of <div>s created by ng-repeat is data bound, the list automatically shrinks when items disappear. Remember, this `remove()` function gets called from the UI whenever the user clicks on one of the Remove buttons.

Up Next

We've looked at just the most basic idioms in Angular and some very simple examples. The rest of the book is dedicated to showing off what the framework has to offer.

CHAPTER 2

Anatomy of an AngularJS Application

Unlike typical libraries where you pick and choose functions as you like, everything in Angular is designed to be used as a collaborative suite. In this chapter we'll cover all of the basic building blocks in Angular so you can understand how they fit together. Many of these blocks will be covered in more detail in later chapters.

Invoking Angular

Any application must do two things to start Angular:

1. Load the *angular.js* library
2. Tell Angular which part of the DOM it should manage with the `ng-app` directive

Loading the Script

Loading the library is straightforward and follows the same rules as any other JavaScript library. You can load the script from Google's content delivery network (CDN), like so:

```
<script
    src="https://ajax.googleapis.com/ajax/libs/angularjs/1.0.4/angular.min.js">
</script>
```

Using Google's CDN is recommended. Google's servers are fast, and the script is cacheable across applications. That is, if your user has multiple apps that use Angular, she'll have to download only it once. Also, if the user has visited other sites that use the Google CDN link for Angular, she won't need to download it again when visiting your site.

If you prefer to host locally (or anywhere else), you can do that too. Just specify the correct location in the `src`.

Declaring Angular's Boundaries with ng-app

The `ng-app` directive lets you tell Angular which part of your page it should expect to manage. If you're building an all-Angular application, you should include `ng-app` as part of the `<html>` tag, like so:

```
<html ng-app>
  ...
</html>
```

This tells Angular to manage all DOM elements in the page.

If you've got an existing app where some other technology expects to manage the DOM, such as Java or Rails, you can tell Angular to manage only a part of the page by placing it on some element like a `<div>` within the page.

```
<html>
  ...
  <div ng-app>
    ...
  </div>
  ...
</html>
```

Model View Controller

In Chapter 1, we mentioned that Angular supports the Model View Controller style of application design. Though you have a lot of flexibility in designing your Angular app, you will always have some flavor of:

- A model containing data that represents the current state of your application.
- Views that display this data.
- Controllers that manage the relationship between your model and your views.

You'll create your model using object attributes, or even just primitive types containing your data. There's nothing special about model variables. If you want to display some text to the user, you could have a string, like so:

```
var someText = 'You have started your journey.';
```

You create your views by writing a template as an HTML page and merging it with data from your model. As we've seen, you can insert a placeholder in the DOM and set its text like this:

```
<p>{{someText}}</p>
```

We call this double-curly syntax interpolation, as it inserts new content into an existing template.

The controllers are classes or types you write to tell Angular which objects or primitives make up your model by assigning them to the $scope object passed into your controller:

```
function TextController($scope) {
  $scope.someText = someText;
}
```

Bringing it all together, we have:

```
<html ng-app>
<body ng-controller="TextController">
  <p>{{someText}}</p>

  <script
      src="https://ajax.googleapis.com/ajax/libs/angularjs/1.0.1/angular.min.js">
  </script>

  <script>
    function TextController($scope) {
      $scope.someText = 'You have started your journey.';
    }
  </script>
</body>
</html>
```

Loading this in a browser, you would see:

```
You have started your journey.
```

Though this primitive-style model works in simple cases, for most applications you'll want to create a model object to contain your data. We'll create a messages model object and use it to store our someText. So instead of:

```
var someText = 'You have started your journey.';
```

you would write:

```
var messages = {};
messages.someText = 'You have started your journey.';
function TextController($scope) {
  $scope.messages = messages;
}
```

and use it in your template as:

```
<p>{{messages.someText}}</p>
```

As we'll see later when we discuss the $scope object, creating a model object like this will prevent unexpected behavior that could be caused by the prototypal inheritance in $scope objects.

While we're discussing practices that will save you in the long run, in the previous example, we've created TextController in the global scope. While this is fine for examples, the right way to define a controller is as part of something called a module, which provides a namespace for related parts of your application. The updated code would look like the following:

```
<html ng-app='myApp'>
<body ng-controller='TextController'>
  <p>{{someText.message}}</p>

<script
    src="https://ajax.googleapis.com/ajax/libs/angularjs/1.0.1/angular.min.js">
</script>

<script>
  var myAppModule = angular.module('myApp', []);

  myAppModule.controller('TextController',
      function($scope) {
    var someText = {};
    someText.message = 'You have started your journey.';
    $scope.someText = someText;
  });
</script>
</body>
</html>
```

In this version, we told our ng-app element about the name of our module, *myApp*. We then called the Angular object to create a module named *myApp* and pass our controller's function to a call to that module's controller function.

We'll get to all the whys and hows of modules in a bit. For now, just remember that keeping things out of the global namespace is a good thing and that modules are the mechanism we use to do so.

Templates and Data Binding

Templates in Angular applications are just HTML documents that we load from the server or define in a <script> tag like any other static resource. You define your UI in the template, using standard HTML plus Angular directives where you need UI components.

Once in the web browser, Angular expands these templates into your full application by merging your template with data. We saw an example of this in Chapter 1 when we displayed a list of items in the shopping cart:

```
<div ng-repeat="item in items">
  <span>{{item.title}}</span>
  ...
</div>
```

Here, it stamps out a copy of the outer <div>, and everything inside it, once for every element in the items array.

So where does this data come from? In our shopping cart example, we just defined it in an array in our code. This works great for when you're starting to build a UI and just want to test out how it will work. Most apps, however, will use some persistent data source on the server. Your app in the browser connects to your server and requests whatever it needs for the page the user is on, and Angular merges it with your template.

The basic startup flow looks like this:

1. A user requests the first page of your application.
2. The user's browser makes an HTTP connection to your server and loads the `in dex.html` page containing your template.
3. Angular loads into the page, waits for the page to be fully loaded, and then looks for `ng-app` to define its template boundaries.
4. Angular traverses the template and looks for directives and bindings. This results in registration of listeners and DOM manipulation, as well as fetching initial data from the server. The end result of this work is that the app is bootstrapped and the template is converted into view as a DOM.
5. You connect to your server to load additional data you need to show the user as needed.

Steps 1 through 3 are standard for every Angular app. It's in steps 4 and 5 that you have choices. These steps can happen synchronously or asynchronously. For performance, the data your app needs to display to the user on the first view can come down with the HTML template to avoid multiple requests.

By structuring your application with Angular, your application's templates are kept separate from the data that populates them. The result of this is that these templates are now cacheable. Only new data need come down to the browser after the first load. Just as with JavaScript, images, CSS, and other resources, caching these templates can give your application even better performance.

Displaying Text

You can display and update text anywhere in your UI using the `ng-bind` directive. It has two equivalent forms. One we've seen with double-curly braces:

```
<p>{{greeting}}</p>
```

Then there's an attribute-based directive called `ng-bind`:

```
<p ng-bind="greeting"></p>
```

Both are equivalent in their output. If the model variable greeting is set to "Hi there," Angular will generate the HTML:

```
<p>Hi there</p>
```

And the browser will display "Hi there".

So why would you use one form over the other? We created the double-curly interpolation syntax to read more naturally and require less typing. While both forms produce equivalent output, with the double-curly syntax, on the very first page load of your application's *index.html*, there's a chance that your user will see the un-rendered template before Angular has a chance to replace the curlies with your data. Subsequent views won't suffer from this.

The reason is that the browser loads the HTML page, renders it, and only then does Angular get a chance to interpret it as you intended.

The good news is that you can still use {{ }} in the majority of your templates. For the data binding you do in your index.html page, however, use ng-bind instead. That way, your users will see nothing until the data has loaded.

Form Inputs

Working with form elements in Angular is simple. As we've seen in several examples, you can use the ng-model attribute to bind elements to your model properties. This works with all the standard form elements like text inputs, radio buttons, checkboxes, and so on. We can bind a checkbox to a property like so:

```
<form ng-controller="SomeController">
  <input type="checkbox" ng-model="youCheckedIt">
</form>
```

This means that:

1. When the user checks the box, a property called youCheckedIt on the SomeCon troller's $scope will become true. Unchecking the box makes youCheckedIt false.

2. If you set $scope.youCheckedIt to true in SomeController, the box becomes checked in the UI. Setting it to false unchecks the box.

Now let's say we actually want to take action when the user does something. For input elements, you use the ng-change attribute to specify a controller method that should be called whenever the user changes the input's value. Let's do a simple calculator to help startup owners understand how much money they need to get going:

```
<form ng-controller="StartUpController">
  Starting: <input ng-change="computeNeeded()"
                    ng-model="funding.startingEstimate">
  Recommendation: {{funding.needed}}
</form>
```

For our simplistic example, let's just set the output to be ten times the user's estimate. We'll also set a default value of zero to start:

```
function StartUpController($scope) {
  $scope.funding = { startingEstimate: 0 };

  $scope.computeNeeded = function() {
    $scope.needed = $scope.startingEstimate * 10;
  };
}
```

There is, however, a potential problem with the strategy in the preceding code. The issue is that we're only recomputing the needed amount when users type in the input field. This works fine if this input field is only ever updated when users type in this particular input. But what if other inputs bind to this property in the model? What if it gets updated when data comes in from the server?

To update the field no matter how it gets updated, we want to use a $scope function called $watch(). We'll talk about watch in detail later in this chapter. The basics are that you can call $watch() with an expression to observe and a callback that gets invoked whenever that expression changes.

In this case, we want to watch funding.startingEstimate and call computeNeeded() whenever it changes. We could then rewrite the StartUpController to use this technique:

```
function StartUpController($scope) {
  $scope.funding = { startingEstimate: 0 };

  computeNeeded = function() {
    $scope.funding.needed = $scope.funding.startingEstimate * 10;
  };

  $scope.$watch('funding.startingEstimate', computeNeeded);
}
```

Note that the expression to watch is in quotes. Yes, it is a string. This string is evaluated as something called an Angular expression. Expressions can do simple operations and have access to the properties in the $scope object. We'll cover expressions more later in this chapter.

You could also watch the return value of a function, but it won't work to watch the property funding.startingEstimate as this evaluates to zero, its initial value, and that zero never changes.

Then, because our funding.needed will automatically update whenever funding.startingEstimate changes, we can write a simpler template, like so:

```
<form ng-controller="StartUpController">
  Starting: <input ng-model="funding.startingEstimate">
  Recommendation: {{funding.needed}}
</form>
```

There are some cases where you don't want to take action on every change; instead, you want to wait until the user tells you he's ready. Examples might be completing a purchase or sending a chat message.

If you have a form that groups inputs, you can use the ng-submit directive on the form itself to specify a function to call when the form submits. We can extend our previous example to let the user request funding for her startup by clicking a button:

```
<form ng-submit="requestFunding()" ng-controller="StartUpController">
  Starting: <input ng-change="computeNeeded()" ng-model="startingEstimate">
  Recommendation: {{needed}}
  <button>Fund my startup!</button>
</form>

function StartUpController($scope) {
  $scope.computeNeeded = function() {
    $scope.needed = $scope.startingEstimate * 10;
  };

  $scope.requestFunding = function() {
    window.alert("Sorry, please get more customers first.");
  };
}
```

The ng-submit directive also automatically prevents the browser from doing its default POST action when it tries to submit the form.

To handle other event cases, like when you want to provide interactions that don't submit a form, Angular provides event-handling directives that resemble the browser's native event attributes. For onclick, you'd use ng-click. For ondblclick, use ng-dblclick, and so on.

We can try this out by extending our startup calculator one last time with a reset button that will reset the input value to zero:

```
<form ng-submit="requestFunding()" ng-controller="StartUpController">
  Starting: <input ng-change="computeNeeded()" ng-model="startingEstimate">
  Recommendation: {{needed}}
  <button>Fund my startup!</button>
  <button ng-click="reset()">Reset</button>
</form>

function StartUpController($scope) {
  $scope.computeNeeded = function() {
    $scope.needed = $scope.startingEstimate * 10;
  };

  $scope.requestFunding = function() {
    window.alert("Sorry, please get more customers first.");
  };

  $scope.reset = function() {
```

```
    $scope.startingEstimate = 0;
  };
}
```

A Few Words on Unobtrusive JavaScript

At some point in your JavaScript development career, someone probably told you that you should be writing "unobtrusive JavaScript," and that using click, mousedown, and other such inline event handlers in your HTML was a bad idea. He was right.

The idea of unobtrusive JavaScript has been interpreted many ways, but the rationale for this style of coding is something along the following lines:

1. Not everyone's browser supports JavaScript. Let everyone see all of your content and use your app without needing to execute code in the browser.

2. Some folks use browsers that work differently. Visually impaired folks who use screen-readers and some mobile phone users can't use sites with JavaScript.

3. Javascript works differently across different platforms. IE is usually the culprit here. You need to put in different event-handling code depending on the browser.

4. These event handlers reference functions in the global namespace. It will cause you headaches when you try to integrate other libraries with functions of the same names.

5. These event handlers combine structure and behavior. This makes your code more difficult to maintain, extend, and understand.

In most ways, life was better when you wrote JavaScript in this style. One thing that was not better, however, was code complexity and readability. Instead of declaring your event handler actions with the element they act on, you usually had to assign IDs to these elements, get a reference to the element, and set up event handlers with callbacks. You could invent a structure to only create these associations in well-known locations, but most apps ended up with these handler setups littered all over.

In Angular, we decided to reexamine the problem.

The world has changed since these concepts were born. Point #1 is no longer true for any interesting population. If you're running a browser without JavaScript, you're relegated to sites created in the 1990s. As for point #2, modern screen-readers have caught up. With proper use of ARIA semantic tags, you can make very rich UIs easily accessible. Mobile phones now run JavaScript on par with desktop machines.

So now the question is: could we solve #3 and #4 while regaining the readability and simplicity of the inline technique?

As previously mentioned, for most inline event handlers, Angular has an equivalent in the form of ng-eventhandler="expression" where eventhandler would be replaced by `click`, `mousedown`, `change`, and so on. If you want to get notified when a user clicks on an element, you simply use the `ng-click` directive like this:

```
<div ng-click="doSomething()">...</div>
```

Is your brain saying "No, no, no! Bad, bad, bad!"? The good news is that you can relax. These directives differ from their event handler predecessors in that they:

- Behave the same in every browser. Angular takes care of the differences for you.
- Do not operate on the global namespace. The expressions you specify can only access functions and data that is in the scope of the element's controller.

This last point may sound a little cryptic, so let's look at an example. In a typical app, you would create a nav bar and a content area that changes as you select different menu options from the nav. We could write the skeleton for it, like so:

```
<div class="navbar" ng-controller="NavController">
...
  <li class="menu-item" ng-click="doSomething()">Something</li>
...
</div>

<div class="contentArea" ng-controller="ContentAreaController">
...
  <div ng-click="doSomething()">...</div>
...
</div>
```

Here both the `<li>` in the navbar and the `<div>` in the content area call a function called `doSomething()` when a user clicks on them. As the developer, you set up the function that these calls refer to in your controller code. They could be the same function or different ones:

```
function NavController($scope) {
  $scope.doSomething = doA;
}

function ContentAreaController($scope) {
  $scope.doSomething = doB;
}
```

Here, `doA()` and `doB()` functions can be the same or different, as you define them.

We're now left with point #5, combining structure and behavior. This is a hand-wavy argument, as you can't point to any concrete negative outcomes, but it's very similar to a real problem we had in mind, combining responsibilities of the presentation and your application logic. This certainly does have the negative side effects that folks talk about when describing the issue labeled as structure/behavior.

There's a simple acid test we can use to figure out if our system suffers from this coupling: can we create a unit test for our app logic that doesn't require the DOM to be present?

In Angular, yes we can write controllers containing our business logic without having references to the DOM. The problem was never in the event handlers, but rather in the way we needed to write JavaScript previously. Notice that in all the controllers we've written so far, here and elsewhere in this book, there are no references to the DOM or DOM events anywhere. You can easily create these controllers without the DOM. All of the work of locating elements and handling events happens within Angular.

This matters first when writing unit tests. If you need the DOM, you have to create it in your test setup, adding to your test complexity. There's more maintenance because when your page changes, you need to change the DOM for your tests. Finally, DOM access is slow. Slow tests mean slow feedback and eventually slow releases. Angular controller tests have none of these problems.

So there you go. You can happily use declarative event handlers with simplicity and readability, without the guilt of violating best practices.

Lists, Tables, and Other Repeated Elements

Possibly the most useful Angular directive, ng-repeat creates a copy of a set of elements once for every item in a collection. You should use it everywhere you want to create lists of things.

Let's say we're writing a student roster application for teachers. We'd likely get the student data from a server, but for this example let's just define it as a model in JavaScript:

```
var students = [{name:'Mary Contrary', id:'1'},
                {name:'Jack Sprat', id:'2'},
                {name:'Jill Hill', id:'3'}];

function StudentListController($scope) {
  $scope.students = students;
}
```

To display this list of students, we can do something like the following:

```
<ul ng-controller=''>
  <li ng-repeat='student in students'>
    <a href='/student/view/{{student.id}}'>{{student.name}}</a>
  </li>
</ul>
```

The ng-repeat will make a copy of all of the HTML inside the tag, including the tag it's placed on. With this, we would see:

- Mary Contrary
- Jack Sprat

- Jill Hill

…linking to */student/view/1*, */student/view/2*, and */student/view/3*, respectively.

As we've seen before, changing the student's array will automatically change the rendered list. If we were to do something like inserting a new student into the list:

```
var students = [{name:'Mary Contrary', id:'1'},
                {name:'Jack Sprat', id:'2'},
                {name:'Jill Hill', id:'3'}];

function StudentListController($scope) {
  $scope.students = students;

  $scope.insertTom = function () {
    $scope.students.splice(1, 0, {name:'Tom Thumb', id:'4'});
  };
}
```

and adding a button to invoke it in the template:

```
<ul ng-controller=''>
  <li ng-repeat='student in students'>
    <a href='/student/view/{{student.id}}'>{{student.name}}</a>
  </li>
</ul>
<button ng-click="insertTom()">Insert</button>
```

we now see:

- Mary Contrary
- Tom Thumb
- Jack Sprat
- Jill Hill

The `ng-repeat` directive also gives you references to the index of the current element via `$index`, and booleans that tell you if you're on the first element, somewhere in the middle, or the last element of the collection with `$first`, `$middle`, and `$last`.

You might imagine using the `$index` to label rows in a table. Given a template like this:

```
<table ng-controller='AlbumController'>
  <tr ng-repeat='track in album'>
    <td>{{$index + 1}}</td>
    <td>{{track.name}}</td>
    <td>{{track.duration}}</td>
  </tr>
</table>
```

and this controller:

```
var album = [{name:'Southwest Serenade', duration: '2:34'},
             {name:'Northern Light Waltz', duration: '3:21'},
             {name:'Eastern Tango', duration: '17:45'}];

function AlbumController($scope) {
  $scope.album = album;
}
```

We get the following:

1 Southwest Serenade 2:34

2 Northern Light Waltz 3:21

3 Eastern Tango 17:45

Hiding and Showing

For menus, context-sensitive tools, and many other cases, showing and hiding elements is a key feature. As with everything else in Angular, we drive UI changes based on change in a model, and reflect that change into the UI through directives.

Here, it's ng-show and ng-hide that do our work. They provide equivalent but inverse functionality for showing and hiding based on the expression you pass to them. That is, ng-show will show its element when its expression is true and hide it when false. The ng-hide hides when true and shows when false. You should use whichever makes more sense to express your intention.

These directives work by setting the element styles to display:block to show and display:none to hide as appropriate. Let's take a fictitious example where we're building the control panel for a Death Ray.

```
<div ng-controller='DeathrayMenuController'>
  <button ng-click='toggleMenu()'>Toggle Menu</button>
  <ul ng-show='menuState.show'>
    <li ng-click='stun()'>Stun</li>
    <li ng-click='disintegrate()'>Disintegrate</li>
    <li ng-click='erase()'>Erase from history</li>
  </ul>
<div/>
function DeathrayMenuController($scope) {
  $scope.menuState.show = false;

  $scope.toggleMenu = function() {
    $scope.menuState.show = !$scope.menuState.show;
  };

  // death ray functions left as exercise to reader
}
```

CSS Classes and Styles

It may be obvious by now that you can dynamically set classes and styles in your application just by data binding them using the {{ }} interpolation notation. You can even compose partial class name matches in your templates. If, for example, you want to conditionally disable some menus, you might do something like the following to visually indicate it to your user:

Given this CSS:

```
.menu-disabled-true {
  color: gray;
}
```

you could show the stun function of your DeathRay as disabled with this template:

```
<div ng-controller='DeathrayMenuController'>
  <ul>
    <li class='menu-disabled-{{isDisabled}}' ng-click='stun()'>Stun</li>
    ...
  </ul>
<div/>
```

where you'd set the isDisabled property via your controller as appropriate:

```
function DeathrayMenuController($scope) {
  $scope.isDisabled = false;

  $scope.stun = function() {
    // stun the target, then disable menu to allow regeneration
    $scope.isDisabled = 'true';
  };
}
```

The class on the stun menu item will be set to menu-disabled- plus the value of $scope.isDisabled. As this is initially false, the result will be menu-disabled-false. As there's no CSS rule that matches, there will be no effect. When $scope.isDisabled is set to true, the CSS rule becomes menu-disabled-true, which invokes the rule to make the text gray.

This technique works equally well when combining inline styles with interpolation, such as with style="{{some expression}}".

While kind of clever, this technique has the drawback of using a level of indirection in composing your class names. While you can easily understand it in this small example, it can quickly become unmanageable having to read both your template and JavaScript to correctly create your CSS.

Because of this, Angular provides the ng-class and ng-style directives. Each of them takes an expression. The result of evaluating this expression can be one of the following:

- A string representing space-delimited class names
- An array of class names
- A map of class names to boolean values

Let's imagine that you want to display errors and warnings to your users in a standard location in the application's header. Using the ng-class directive, you could do something like this:

```
.error {
  background-color: red;
}

.warning {
  background-color: yellow;
}
<div ng-controller='HeaderController'>
  ...
  <div ng-class='{error: isError, warning: isWarning}'>{{messageText}}</div>
  ...
  <button ng-click='showError()'>Simulate Error</button>
  <button ng-click='showWarning()'>Simulate Warning</button>
</div>
function HeaderController($scope) {
  $scope.isError = false;
  $scope.isWarning = false;

  $scope.showError = function() {
    $scope.messageText = 'This is an error!';
    $scope.isError = true;
    $scope.isWarning = false;
  };

  $scope.showWarning = function() {
    $scope.messageText = 'Just a warning.  Please carry on.';
    $scope.isWarning = true;
    $scope.isError = false;
  };
}
```

You can even do nifty things like highlighting a selected row in a table. Let's say we're building a restaurant directory and we want to highlight a row that the user clicks on.

In our CSS, we set up the style for a highlighted row:

```
.selected {
  background-color: lightgreen;
}
```

In the template, we set ng-class to {selected: $index==selectedRow}. This has the effect of setting the selected class when our model property called selectedRow matches the ng-repeat's $index. We'll also set up an ng-click to notify our controller as to which row the user clicks:

```
<table ng-controller='RestaurantTableController'>
  <tr ng-repeat='restaurant in directory' ng-click='selectRestaurant($index)'
      ng-class='{selected: $index==selectedRow}'>
    <td>{{restaurant.name}}</td>
    <td>{{restaurant.cuisine}}</td>
  </tr>
</table>
```

In our JavaScript, we just set up some dummy restaurants and create the selectRow function:

```
function RestaurantTableController($scope) {
  $scope.directory = [{name:'The Handsome Heifer', cuisine:'BBQ'},
                      {name:'Green's Green Greens', cuisine:'Salads'},
                      {name:'House of Fine Fish', cuisine:'Seafood'}];

  $scope.selectRestaurant = function(row) {
    $scope.selectedRow = row;
  };
}
```

Considerations for src and href Attributes

When data binding to an <img> or <a> tag, the obvious path of using {{ }} in the src or href attributes won't work well. Because browsers are aggressive about loading images parallel to other content, Angular doesn't get a chance to intercept data binding requests. While the obvious syntax for an <img> might be:

```
<img src="/images/cats/{{favoriteCat}}">
```

Instead, you should use the ng-src attribute and write your template as:

```
<img ng-src="/images/cats/{{favoriteCat}}">
```

Similarly, for the <a> tag, you should use ng-href:

```
<a ng-href="/shop/category={{numberOfBalloons}}">some text</a>
```

Expressions

The goal behind the expressions that you use in templates is to let you be as clever as you need to be to create hooks between your template, your application logic, and your data, but at the same time prevent application logic from sneaking into the template.

Until this point, we've been mostly using references to data primitives as the expressions passed to Angular directives. But these expressions can do much more. You can do simple math (+, -, /, *, %), make comparisons (==, !=, >, <, >=, ⇐), perform boolean logic (&&, ||, !) and bitwise operations (\^, &, |). You can call functions you expose on $scope in your controller and you can reference arrays and object notation ([ ], { }, .).

All of these are valid examples of expressions:

```
<div ng-controller='SomeController'>
  <div>{{recompute() / 10}}</div>
  <ul ng-repeat='thing in things'>
    <li ng-class='{highlight: $index % 4 >= threshold($index)}'>
      {{otherFunction($index)}}
    </li>
  </ul>
</div>
```

The first expression here, `recompute() / 10`, while valid, is a good example of putting logic in the template, and should be avoided. Keeping a separation of responsibilities between your view and controllers ensures that they're easy to reason and easy to test.

While you can do quite a lot with expressions, they are computed with a custom parser that's part of Angular. They are not evaluated using JavaScript's `eval()`, and are considerably more restrictive.

Instead, they are evaluated using a custom parser that comes with Angular. In it, you won't find looping constructs (for, while, and so on), flow-of-control operators (if-else, throw) or operators that modify data (++, --). When you need these types of operations, do them in your controller or via a directive.

Though expressions are more restrictive than JavaScript in many ways, they are more forgiving to `undefined` and `null`. Instead of throwing a `NullPointerException` error, templates will simply render nothing. This allows you to safely use model values that haven't been set yet, and have them appear in the UI as soon as they get populated.

Separating UI Responsibilities with Controllers

Controllers have three responsibilities in your app:

- Set up the initial state in your application's model
- Expose model and functions to the view (UI template) through $scope
- Watch other parts of the model for changes and take action

We've seen many examples of the first two in this chapter already. We'll get to that last one in a bit. The conceptual purpose of controllers, however, is to provide the code or logic to execute the user's wishes as they interact with the view.

To keep your controllers small and manageable, our recommendation is that you create one controller per functional area in your view. That is, if you have a menu, create a

`MenuController`. If you have a navigational breadcrumb, write a `BreadcrumbControl ler`, and so on.

You're probably starting to get the picture, but to be explicit, controllers are tied to a specific piece of the DOM that they're in charge of managing. The two main ways of associating a controller with a DOM node are specifying it in the template by declaring it in an `ng-controller` attribute, and associating it with a dynamically loadable DOM template fragment, called a *view*, through a *route*.

We'll talk about views and routes later in this chapter.

If you have complex sections of your UI, you can keep your code simple and maintainable, by creating nested controllers that can share model and functions through an inheritance tree. Nesting controllers is simple; you do it by simply assigning a controller to a DOM element that is inside another one, like so:

```
<div ng-controller="ParentController">
  <div ng-controller="ChildController">...</div>
</div>
```

Though we express this as nested controllers, the actual nesting happens in scopes. The `$scope` passed to a nested controller prototypically inherits from its parent controller's `$scope`. In this case, this means that the `$scope` passed to `ChildController` will have access to all the properties of the `$scope` passed to `ParentController`.

Publishing Model Data with Scopes

The `$scope` object passed to our controllers is the mechanism we use to expose model data to views. You may have other data in your application, but Angular only considers it part of the model when it can reach these properties through a scope. You can think of scopes as a context that you use to make changes to your model observable.

We've seen many examples of setting up scopes explicitly, as in `$scope.count = 5`. There are also some indirect ways to set up the model from the template itself. You can do so in the following ways:

1. Through an expression. Since expressions execute in the context of the controller's scope associated with their element, setting properties in expressions is the same as setting a property of the controller's scope. That is, doing this:

   ```
   <button ng-click='count=3'>Set count to three</button>
   ```

   has the same effect as doing this:

   ```
   <div ng-controller='CountController'>
     <button ng-click='setCount()'>Set count to three</button>
   </div>
   ```

   with your `CountController` defined as:

```
function CountController($scope) {
  $scope.setCount = function() {
    $scope.count=3;
  }
}
```

2. Using ng-model on a form input. As with expressions, the model specified as the argument for ng-model also works within the scope of the enclosing controller. The one addition is that this creates a bi-directional data binding between the form field state and your specified model.

Observing Model Changes with $watch

Possibly the most used of all scope functions is $watch, which notifies you when parts of your model change. You can watch individual object properties and computed results (functions), really anything that could be accessed as a property or computed as a Java-Script function. The function's signature is:

```
$watch(watchFn, watchAction, deepWatch)
```

The details of each parameter are as follows:

watchFn

This parameter is a string with an Angular expression or a function that returns the current value of the model that you want to watch. This expression will be evaluated multiple times, so you need to make sure that it has no side effects. That is, it can be called multiple times without changing state. For the same reason, watch expressions should be computationally cheap. If you've passed in an Angular expression in a string, it will be evaluated against objects available to the scope it's called on.

watchAction

This is the function or expression to be called when the watchFn changes. In the function form, it receives the new and old values of watchFn as well as a reference to the scope. Its signature is function(newValue, oldValue, scope).

deepWatch

If set to true, this optional boolean parameter tells Angular to examine each property within the watched object for changes. You'd use this if you wanted to watch individual elements in an array or properties in an object instead of just a simple value. As Angular needs to walk the array or object, this can be computationally expensive if the collection is large.

The $watch function returns a function that will de-register the listener when you no longer want to receive change notifications.

If we wanted to watch a property and then later de-register it, we would use the following:

```
...
var dereg = $scope.$watch('someModel.someProperty', callbackOnChange());
...
dereg();
```

Let's revisit our shopping cart scenario from Chapter 1 for a full example. Let's say that we want to apply a $10 discount when the customer adds more than $100 worth of merchandise to her cart. For a template, we'll use:

```
<div ng-controller="CartController">
  <div ng-repeat="item in items">
    <span>{{item.title}}</span>
    <input ng-model="item.quantity">
    <span>{{item.price | currency}}</span>
    <span>{{item.price * item.quantity | currency}}</span>
  </div>
  <div>Total: {{totalCart() | currency}}</div>
  <div>Discount: {{bill.discount | currency}}</div>
  <div>Subtotal: {{subtotal() | currency}}</div>
</div>
```

With a CartController, it would look like the following:

```
function CartController($scope) {
  $scope.bill = {};

  $scope.items = [
    {title: 'Paint pots', quantity: 8, price: 3.95},
    {title: 'Polka dots', quantity: 17, price: 12.95},
    {title: 'Pebbles', quantity: 5, price: 6.95}
  ];

  $scope.totalCart = function() {
    var total = 0;
    for (var i = 0, len = $scope.items.length; i < len; i++) {
      total = total + $scope.items[i].price * $scope.items[i].quantity;
    }

    return total;
  }

  $scope.subtotal = function() {
    return $scope.totalCart() - $scope.discount;
  };

  function calculateDiscount(newValue, oldValue, scope) {
    $scope.bill.discount = newValue > 100 ? 10 : 0;
  }

  $scope.$watch($scope.totalCart, calculateDiscount);
}
```

Notice that at the bottom of `CartController`, we've set up a watch on the value of `totalCart()` which we use to sum up the total price for this purchase. Whenever this value changes, the watch will call `calculateDiscount()`, and we get to set the discount to an appropriate value. If the total is $100, we'll set the discount to $10. Otherwise, the discount will be $0.

You can see how this example would look to a user in Figure 2-1.

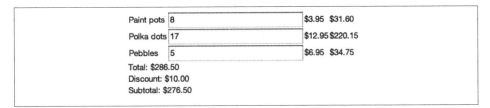

Figure 2-1. Shopping cart with discount

Performance Considerations in watch()

The preceding example executes correctly, but there is a potential problem with performance. Though it isn't obvious, if you put a debugger breakpoint in `totalCart()`, you'd see that it gets called six times to render this page. Though you'd never notice it in this application, in more complex apps, running it six times could be an issue.

Why six? Three of them we can trace pretty easily, as it runs one time each in:

- The template as `{{totalCart() | currency}}`
- The `subtotal()` function
- The `$watch()` function

Then Angular runs all of these again, bringing us to six. Angular does this to verify that transitive changes in your model have fully propagated and your model has *settled*. Angular does this checking by making a copy of all watched properties and comparing them to the current value to see if they've changed. In fact, Angular may run this up to ten times to ensure full propagation. If changes are still occurring after ten iterations, Angular exits with an error. If that occurs, you probably have a dependency loop that you'll need to fix.

Though you currently need to worry about this, by the time you've finished this book it may be a non-issue. While Angular has had to implement data binding in JavaScript, we've been working with the TC39 folks on a low-level native implementation called `Object.observe()` (*http://updates.html5rocks.com/2012/11/Respond-to-change-with-Object-observe*). With this in place, Angular will automatically use `Object.observe()` wherever present to give you native-speed data binding.

As you'll see in the next chapter, Angular has a nice Chrome debugging extension called Batarang that will automatically highlight expensive data bindings for you.

Now that we know about this issue, there are a few ways we can solve it. One way would be to create a $watch on changes to the items array and just recalculate the total, discount, and subtotal as properties on the $scope.

To do this, we'd update the template to use these properties:

```
<div>Total: {{bill.total | currency}}</div>
<div>Discount: {{bill.discount | currency}}</div>
<div>Subtotal: {{bill.subtotal | currency}}</div>
```

Then, in JavaScript, we'd watch the items array, and call a function to calculate the totals on any change to that array, like so:

```
function CartController($scope) {
  $scope.bill = {};

  $scope.items = [
    {title: 'Paint pots', quantity: 8, price: 3.95},
    {title: 'Polka dots', quantity: 17, price: 12.95},
    {title: 'Pebbles', quantity: 5, price: 6.95}
  ];

  var calculateTotals = function() {
    var total = 0;
    for (var i = 0, len = $scope.items.length; i < len; i++) {
      total = total + $scope.items[i].price * $scope.items[i].quantity;
    }
    $scope.bill.totalCart = total;
    $scope.bill.discount = total > 100 ? 10 : 0;
    $scope.bill.subtotal = total - $scope.bill.discount;
  };

  $scope.$watch('items', calculateTotals, true);
}
```

Notice here that the $watch specified items as a string. This is possible because the $watch function can take either a function (as we did previously) or a string. If a string is passed to the $watch function, then it will be evaluated as an expression in the scope of the $scope it's called on.

This strategy might work well for your app. However, since we're watching the items array, Angular will have to make a copy of it to compare it for us. For a large list of items, it may perform better if we just recalculate the bill properties every time Angular evaluates the page. We can do this by creating a $watch with only a watchFn that will recalculate our properties like this:

```
$scope.$watch(function() {
  var total = 0;
```

```
    for (var i = 0; i < $scope.items.length; i++) {
      total = total + $scope.items[i].price * $scope.items[i].quantity;
    }
    $scope.bill.totalCart = total;
    $scope.bill.discount = total > 100 ? 10 : 0;
    $scope.bill.subtotal = total - $scope.bill.discount;
});
```

Watching multiple things

What if you want to watch multiple properties or objects and execute a function whenever any of them change? You'd have two basic options:

- Put them into an array or object and pass in deepWatch as true.
- Watch a concatenated value of the properties.

In the first case, if you've got an object with two properties *a* and *b* in your scope, and want to execute the callMe() function on change, you could watch both of them, like so:

```
$scope.$watch('things.a + things.b', callMe(...));
```

Of course, *a* and *b* could be on different objects, and you could make the list as long as you like. If the list is long, you would likely write a function that returns the concatenated value rather than relying on an expression for the logic.

In the second case, you might want to watch all the properties on the things object. In this case, you could do this:

```
$scope.$watch('things', callMe(...), true);
```

Here, passing in *true* as the third parameter asks Angular to walk the properties of things and call callMe() on a change to any of them. This works equally well on an array as it does here on an object.

Organizing Dependencies with Modules

In any non-trivial application, figuring out how to organize the functionality of your code into areas of responsibility is often a hard task. We've seen how controllers give us a place to put the code that exposes the right data and functions to the view template. But what about the rest of the code we need to support our applications? The most obvious place to put this would be in functions on the controllers.

This works fine for small apps and the examples that we've seen so far, but it quickly becomes unmanageable in real apps. The controllers would become a dumping ground for everything and anything we need to do. They'd be hard to understand and likely hard to change.

Enter modules. They provide a way to group dependencies for a functional area within your application, and a mechanism to automatically resolve dependencies (also known as dependency injection). Generically, we call these dependencies services, as they provide specific services to our application.

For example, if in our shopping website a controller needs to get a list of items for sale from the server, we'd want some object—let's call it Items—to take care of getting the items from the server. The Items object, in turn, needs some way to communicate with the database on the server over XHR or WebSockets.

Doing this without modules looks something like this:

```
function ItemsViewController($scope) {
  // make request to server
  …

  // parse response into Item objects
  …

  // set Items array on $scope so the view can display it
  ...
}
```

While this would certainly work, it has a number of potential problems.

- If some other controller also needs to get Items from the server, we now have to replicate this code. This makes maintenance a burden, as now if we make schema or other changes, we have to update that code in several places.

- With other factors like server authentication, parsing complexity, and so on, it is difficult to reason about the boundaries of responsibility for this controller object, and reading the code is harder.

- To unit test this bit of code, we'd either need to actually have a server running, or monkey patch (*http://en.wikipedia.org/wiki/Monkey_patch*) XMLHttpRequest to return mock data. Having to run the server will make tests very slow, it's a pain to set up, and it usually introduces flakiness into tests. The monkey patching route solves the speed and flakiness problems, but it means you have to remember to un-patch any patched objects between tests, and it brings additional complexity and brittleness by forcing you to specify the exact on-the-wire format for your data (and in having to update the tests whenever this format changes).

With modules, and the dependency injection we get from them, we can write our controller much more simply, like this:

```
function ShoppingController($scope, Items) {
  $scope.items = Items.query();
}
```

You're probably now asking yourself, "Sure, that looks cool, but where does `Items` come from?" The preceding code assumes that we've defined `Items` as a service.

Services are singleton (single-instance) objects that carry out the tasks necessary to support your application's functionality. Angular comes with many services like `$location`, for interacting with the browser's location, `$route`, for switching views based on location (URL) changes, and `$http`, for communicating with servers.

You can, and should, create your own services to do all of the tasks unique to your application. Services can be shared across any controllers that need them. As such, they're a good mechanism to use when you need to communicate across controllers and share state. Angular's bundled services start with a `$`, so while you can name them anything you like, its a good idea to avoid starting them with `$` to avoid naming collisions.

You define services with the module object's API. There are three functions for creating generic services, with different levels of complexity and ability:

Function	Defines
`provider(name, Object OR constructor() )`	A configurable service with complex creation logic. If you pass an Object, it should have a function named `$get` that returns an instance of the service. Otherwise, Angular assumes you've passed a constructor that, when called, creates the instance.
`factory(name, $get Function() )`	A non-configurable service with complex creation logic. You specify a function that, when called, returns the service instance. You could think of this as `provider(name, { $get: $getFunction() } )`.
`service(name, constructor() )`	A non-configurable service with simple creation logic. Like the constructor option with provider, Angular calls it to create the service instance.

We'll look at the configuration option for `provider()` later, but let's discuss an example with `factory()` for our preceding Items example. We can write the service like this:

```
// Create a module to support our shopping views
var shoppingModule = angular.module('ShoppingModule', []);

// Set up the service factory to create our Items interface to the
// server-side database
shoppingModule.factory('Items', function() {
  var items = {};
  items.query = function() {
    // In real apps, we'd pull this data from the server...
    return [
      {title: 'Paint pots', description: 'Pots full of paint', price: 3.95},
      {title: 'Polka dots', description: 'Dots with polka, price: 2.95},
      {title: 'Pebbles', description: 'Just little rocks', price: 6.95}
    ];
  };
  return items;
});
```

When Angular creates the `ShoppingController`, it will pass in `$scope` and the new Items service that we've just defined. This is done by parameter name matching. That is, Angular looks at the function signature for our `ShoppingController` class, and notices that it is asking for an `Items` object. Since we've defined `Items` as a service, it knows where to get it.

The result of looking up these dependencies as strings means that the arguments of injectable functions like controller constructors are order-independent. So instead of this:

```
function ShoppingController($scope, Items) {...}
```

we can write this:

```
function ShoppingController(Items, $scope) {...}
```

and it all still functions as we intended.

To get this to work with our template, we need to tell the `ng-app` directive the name of our module, like the following:

```
<html ng-app='ShoppingModule'>
```

To complete the example, we could implement the rest of the template as:

```
<body ng-controller="ShoppingController">
  <h1>Shop!</h1>
  <table>
      <td>{{item.title}}</td>
      <td>{{item.description}}</td>
      <td>{{item.price | currency}}</td>
    </tr>
  </table>
</div>
```

with a resulting app that looks like Figure 2-2.

Shop!

Paint pots	Pots full of paint	$3.95
Polka dots	Dots with that polka groove	$12.95
Pebbles	Just little rocks, really	$6.95

Figure 2-2. Shop items

How Many Modules Do I Need?

As services themselves can have dependencies, the Module API lets you define dependencies for your dependencies.

In most applications, it will work well enough to create a single module for all the code you create and put all of your dependencies in it. If you use services or directives from third-party libraries, they'll come with their own modules. As your app depends on them, you'd refer to them as dependencies of your application's module.

For instance, if you include the (fictitious) modules SnazzyUIWidgets and SuperData-Sync, your application's module declaration would look like this:

```
var appMod = angular.module('app', ['SnazzyUIWidgets', 'SuperDataSync']);
```

Formatting Data with Filters

Filters allow you to declare how to transform data for display to the user within an interpolation in your template. The syntax for using filters is:

```
{{ expression | filterName : parameter1 : ...parameterN }}
```

where expression is any Angular expression, `filterName` is the name of the filter you want to use, and the parameters to the filter are separated by colons. The parameters themselves can be any valid Angular expression.

Angular comes with several filters, like currency, which we've seen:

```
{{12.9 | currency}}
```

This bit of code will display the following:

$12.90

We put this declaration in the view (rather than in the controller or model) because the dollar sign in front of the number is only important to humans, and not to the logic we use to process the number.

Other filters that come with Angular include date, number, uppercase, and more.

Filters can also be chained with additional pipe symbols in the binding. For example, we can format the previous example for no digits after the decimal by adding the number filter, which takes the number of decimals to round to as a parameter. So:

```
{{12.9 | currency | number:0 }}
```

displays:

$13

You're not limited to the bundled filters, and it is simple to write your own. If we wanted to create a filter that title-cased strings for our headings, for example, we could do so as follows:

```
var homeModule = angular.module('HomeModule', []);
homeModule.filter('titleCase', function() {
  var titleCaseFilter = function(input) {
```

```
    var words = input.split(' ');
    for (var i = 0; i < words.length; i++) {
      words[i] = words[i].charAt(0).toUpperCase() + words[i].slice(1);
    }
    return words.join(' ');
  };
  return titleCaseFilter;
});
```

With a template like this:

```
<body ng-app='HomeModule' ng-controller="HomeController">
  <h1>{{pageHeading | titleCase}}</h1>
</body>
```

and inserting the pageHeading as a model variable via a controller:

```
function HomeController($scope) {
  $scope.pageHeading = 'behold the majesty of your page title';
}
```

we would see something resembling Figure 2-3.

Behold The Majesty Of Your Page Title

Figure 2-3. Title case filter

Changing Views with Routes and $location

Though AJAX apps are technically single-page apps (in the sense that they only load an HTML page on the first request, and then just update areas within the DOM thereafter), we usually have multiple sub-page views that we show or hide from the user, as appropriate.

We can use Angular's $route service to manage this scenario for us. Routes let you specify that, for a given URL that the browser points to, Angular should load and display a template, and instantiate a controller to provide context for the template.

You create routes in your application by calling functions on the $routeProvider service as a configuration block. It goes something like this pseudo-code:

```
var someModule = angular.module('someModule', [...module dependencies...])
someModule.config(function($routeProvider) {
  $routeProvider.
    when('url', {controller:aController, templateUrl:'/path/to/tempate'}).
    when(...other mappings for your app...).
    ...
    otherwise(...what to do if nothing else matches...);
)};
```

The preceding code says that when the browser's URL changes to the specified URL, Angular will load the template in */path/to/template*, and associate the root element of this template with `aController` (as if we'd typed `ng-controller=aController`).

The `otherwise()` call in the last line tells the route where to go if nothing else matches.

Let's put it to use. We're building an email app that will easily win out over Gmail, Hotmail, and all the others. We'll call it…A-Mail. For now, let's start simply. We'll have a first view that displays a list of email messages with a date, title, and the sender. When you click a message, it should show you a new view with the body of that message.

 Due to browser security restrictions, if you're trying the code out your-self, you'll need to serve it from a web server instead of just *file://*. If you have python installed, you could serve it by executing `python -m Sim pleHTTPServer 8888` from your working directory.

For the main template, we'll do something a bit different. Instead of putting everything in the first page loaded, we'll just create a layout template that we'll put our views into. We'll place everything that persists from view to view, like our menus, here. In this case, we'll just display a heading with the name of our app. We'll then use the `ng-view` directive to tell Angular where we want our views to appear.

index.html

```
<html ng-app="AMail">
  <head>
    <script src="src/angular.js"></script>
    <script src="src/controllers.js"></script>
  </head>
  <body>
    <h1>A-Mail</h1>
    <div ng-view></div>
  </body>
</html>
```

As our view templates will be inserted into the shell we just created, we can write them as partial HTML documents. For the email list, we'll use `ng-repeat` to iterate through a list of messages and render them into a table.

list.html

```
<table>
  <tr>
    <td><strong>Sender</strong></td>
    <td><strong>Subject</strong></td>
    <td><strong>Date</strong></td>
```

```
    </tr>
    <tr ng-repeat='message in messages'>
      <td>{{message.sender}}</td>
      <td><a href='#/view/{{message.id}}'>{{message.subject}}</td>
      <td>{{message.date}}</td>
    </tr>
  </table>
```

Notice here that we're going to let the user navigate to a particular message by clicking on the subject. We've data bound the URL to message.id, so clicking on a message with id=1 will take the user to */#/view/1*. We'll use this navigation-by-url, also known as deep-linking, in the message detail view's controller, to make a particular message available to the detail view.

To create this message detail view, we'll create a template that displays properties from a single message object.

detail.html

```
<div><strong>Subject:</strong> {{message.subject}}</div>
<div><strong>Sender:</strong> {{message.sender}}</div>
<div><strong>Date:</strong> {{message.date}}</div>
<div>
    <strong>To:</strong>
    <span ng-repeat='recipient in message.recipients'>{{recipient}} </span>
<div>{{message.message}}</div>
<a href='#/'>Back to message list</a>
```

Now, to associate these templates with some controllers, we'll configure the $routePro
vider with the URLs that invoke our controllers and templates.

controllers.js

```
// Create a module for our core AMail services
var aMailServices = angular.module('AMail', []);

// Set up our mappings between URLs, templates, and controllers
function emailRouteConfig($routeProvider) {
  $routeProvider.
  when('/', {
    controller: ListController,
    templateUrl: 'list.html'
  }).
// Notice that for the detail view, we specify a parameterized URL component
// by placing a colon in front of the id
  when('/view/:id', {
    controller: DetailController,
    templateUrl: 'detail.html'
  }).
  otherwise({
    redirectTo: '/'
```

```
    });
  }

  // Set up our route so the AMail service can find it
  aMailServices.config(emailRouteConfig);

  // Some fake emails
  messages = [{
    id: 0, sender: 'jean@somecompany.com', subject: 'Hi there, old friend',
    date: 'Dec 7, 2013 12:32:00', recipients: ['greg@somecompany.com'],
    message: 'Hey, we should get together for lunch sometime and catch up.'
    +'There are many things we should collaborate on this year.'
  }, {
    id: 1,  sender: 'maria@somecompany.com',
    subject: 'Where did you leave my laptop?',
    date: 'Dec 7, 2013 8:15:12', recipients: ['greg@somecompany.com'],
    message: 'I thought you were going to put it in my desk drawer.'
    +'But it does not seem to be there.'
  }, {
    id: 2, sender: 'bill@somecompany.com', subject: 'Lost python',
    date: 'Dec 6, 2013 20:35:02', recipients: ['greg@somecompany.com'],
    message: "Nobody panic, but my pet python is missing from her cage.'
    +'She doesn't move too fast, so just call me if you see her."
  }, ];

  // Publish our messages for the list template
  function ListController($scope) {
    $scope.messages = messages;
  }

  // Get the message id from the route (parsed from the URL) and use it to
  // find the right message object.
  function DetailController($scope, $routeParams) {
    $scope.message = messages[$routeParams.id];
  }
```

We've created the basic structure for an app with many views. We switch views by changing the URL. This means that the forward and back buttons *just work* for users. Users are able to bookmark and email links to views within the app, even though there is only one real HTML page.

Talking to Servers

Okay, enough messing around. Real apps generally talk to real servers. Mobile apps and the emerging Chrome desktop apps may be exceptions, but for everything else, whether you want persistence in the cloud or real-time interactions with other users, you probably want your app to talk to a server.

For this, Angular provides a service called $http. It has an extensive list of abstractions that make it easier to talk to servers. It supports vanilla HTTP, JSONP, and CORS. It includes security provisions to protect from both JSON vulnerabilities and XSRF. It lets you easily transform the request and response data, and it even implements simple caching.

Let's say we want to retrieve products for our shopping site from a server instead of from our silly in-memory mocks. Writing the server bits is beyond the scope of this book, so let's just imagine that we've created a service that will return a list of products as JSON when you make a query to */products*.

Given a response that looks like this:

```
[
  {
    "id": 0,
    "title": "Paint pots",
    "description": "Pots full of paint",
    "price": 3.95
  },
  {
    "id": 1,
    "title": "Polka dots",
    "description": "Dots with that polka groove",
    "price": 12.95
  },
  {
    "id": 2,
    "title": "Pebbles",
    "description": "Just little rocks, really",
    "price": 6.95
  }
  ...etc...
]
```

we could write the query like so:

```
function ShoppingController($scope, $http) {
  $http.get('/products').success(function(data, status, headers, config) {
    $scope.items = data;
  });
}
```

and use it in a template like this:

```
<body ng-controller="ShoppingController">
  <h1>Shop!</h1>
  <table>
    <tr ng-repeat="item in items">
      <td>{{item.title}}</td>
      <td>{{item.description}}</td>
      <td>{{item.price | currency}}</td>
    </tr>
  </table>
```

```
    </div>
  </body>
```

As we learned previously, we would be better off in the long run by delegating the work of talking to the server to a service that could be shared across controllers. We'll take a look at this structure and the full range of $http functions in Chapter 5.

Changing the DOM with Directives

Directives extend HTML syntax, and are the way to associate behavior and DOM transformations with custom elements and attributes. Through them, you can create reusable UI components, configure your application, and do almost anything else you can imagine wanting to do in your UI template.

You can write apps with the built-in directives that come with Angular, but you'll likely run into situations where you want to write your own. You'll know it's time to break into directives when you want to deal with browser events or modify the DOM in a way that isn't already supported by the built-in directives. This code of yours belongs in a directive that you write, and not in a controller, service, or any other place in your app.

As with services, you define directives through the module object's API by calling its directive() function, where directiveFunction is a factory function that defines your directive's features.

```
var appModule = angular.module('appModule', [...]);
appModule.directive('directiveName', directiveFunction);
```

Writing the directive factory function is a deep area, and we've dedicated an entire chapter to it in this book. To whet your appetite, though, let's look at a simple example.

HTML5 has a great new attribute called autofocus that will place keyboard focus on an input element. You'd use it to let the user start interacting with the element via his keyboard without having to click on it first. This is great, as it lets you declaratively specify what you want the browser to do without having to write any JavaScript. But what if you wanted to place focus on some non-input element, like a link or any div? And what if you wanted it to work on non-HTML5 browsers as well? We could do it with a directive.

```
var appModule = angular.module('app', []);

appModule.directive('ngbkFocus', function() {
  return {
    link: function(scope, element, attrs, controller) {
      element[0].focus();
    }
  };
});
```

Here, we're returning the directive configuration object with its link function specified. The link function gets a reference to the enclosing scope, the DOM element it lives on, an array of any attributes passed to the directive, and the controller on the DOM element, if it exists. Here, we only need to get at the element and call its focus() method.

We can then use it in an example like so:

index.html

```
<html lang='en' ng-app='app'>
...include angular and other scripts...
<body ng-controller="SomeController">
  <button ng-click="clickUnfocused()">
    Not focused
  </button>
  <button ngbk-focus ng-click="clickFocused()">
    I'm very focused!
  </button>
  <div>{{message.text}}</div>
</body>
</html>
```

controllers.js

```
function SomeController($scope) {
  $scope.message = { text: 'nothing clicked yet' };

  $scope.clickUnfocused = function() {
    $scope.message.text = 'unfocused button clicked';
  };

  $scope.clickFocused = function {
    $scope.message.text = 'focus button clicked';
  }
}

var appModule = angular.module('app', ['directives']);
```

When the page loads, the user will see the button labeled "I'm very focused!" with the focus highlight. Hitting the spacebar or the enter key will cause a click and invoke the ng-click, which will set the div text to 'focus button clicked'. Opening this example in a browser, we'd see something that looks like Figure 2-4.

Figure 2-4. Focus directive

Validating User Input

Angular automatically augments <form> elements with several nice features suitable for single-page applications. One of these nice features is that Angular lets you declare valid states for inputs within the form and allow submission only when the entire set of elements is valid.

For example, if we're creating a signup form where we require entering a name and email, but have an optional age field, we can validate several user entries before they are submitted to the server. Loading the example that follows into a browser will display what is shown in Figure 2-5.

Figure 2-5. Form validation

We'd want to make sure the user had entered text in the name fields, that he had entered a properly formed email address, and that if he entered an age, it was valid.

We can do this all in the template, using Angular's extensions to <form> and the various input elements, like this:

```
<h1>Sign Up</h1>
<form name='addUserForm'>
  <div>First name: <input ng-model='user.first' required></div>
  <div>Last name: <input ng-model='user.last' required></div>
  <div>Email: <input type='email' ng-model='user.email' required></div>
  <div>Age: <input type='number'
                    ng-model='user.age'
                    ng-maxlength='3'
                    ng-minlength='1'></div>
  <div><button>Submit</button></div>
</form>
```

Notice that we're using the required attribute and input types for email and number from HTML5 to do our validation on some of the fields. This works great with Angular, and in older non-HTML5 browsers, Angular will polyfill these with directives that perform the same jobs.

We can then add a controller to this to handle the submission by changing the form to reference it.

```
<form name='addUserForm' ng-controller="AddUserController">
```

Inside the controller, we can access the validation state of the form through a property called $valid. Angular will set this to true when all the inputs in the form are valid. We can use this $valid property to do nifty things such as disabling the Submit button when the form isn't completed yet.

We can prevent form submission in an invalid state by adding ng-disabled to the Submit button:

```
<button ng-disabled='!addUserForm.$valid'>Submit</button>
```

Finally, we might want the controller to tell the user she's been successfully added. Our final template would look like:

```
<h1>Sign Up</h1>
<form name='addUserForm' ng-controller="AddUserController">
  <div ng-show='message'>{{message}}</div>
  <div>First name: <input name='firstName' ng-model='user.first' required></div>
  <div>Last name: <input ng-model='user.last' required></div>
  <div>Email: <input type='email' ng-model='user.email' required></div>
  <div>Age: <input type='number'
                  ng-model='user.age'
                  ng-maxlength='3'
                  ng-min='1'></div>
  <div><button ng-click='addUser()'
              ng-disabled='!addUserForm.$valid'>Submit</button>
</ng-form>
```

with controller:

```
function AddUserController($scope) {
  $scope.message = '';

  $scope.addUser = function () {
    // TODO for the reader: actually save user to database...
    $scope.message = 'Thanks, ' + $scope.user.first + ', we added you!';
  };
}
```

Moving On

In the last two chapters, we looked at all the most commonly used features in the Angular framework. For each feature discussed, there are many additional details we have yet to cover. In the next chapter, we'll get you going by examining a typical development workflow.

CHAPTER 3

Developing in AngularJS

By now we have delved a little bit into the cogs that make up AngularJS. We now know how to get data from the user into our application, how to display text, and how to do some funky stuff with validation, filtering, and even changing the DOM. But how do we put it all together?

In this chapter, we will cover:

- How to lay out your AngularJS app for rapid development
- Starting your server to see your AngularJS app in action
- Writing and running your unit and scenario tests using Karma
- Compiling and minifying your AngularJS app for production deployment
- Debugging your AngularJS app using Batarang
- Simplifying your development workflow (from creating new files to running your application and tests)
- Integrating your AngularJS project with RequireJS, a dependency management library

This chapter aims to give you a 20,000-foot view of how to possibly lay out your AngularJS app. We won't go into the actual app itself. That is for Chapter 4, which dives into a sample application that uses and shows off various AngularJS features.

Project Organization

We recommend seeding your project using Yeoman (*http://yeoman.io/*), which will create all the necessary files to bootstrap your AngularJS application.

Yeoman is a robust tool comprised of multiple frameworks and client-side libraries. It provides a rapid development environment by automating some routine tasks needed to bootstrap and develop your application. We'll go through a whole section on how to install and use Yeoman this chapter, but until then, we will briefly touch upon Yeoman commands as alternatives to manually performing those operations.

We will also detail the various pieces involved in case you decide not to use Yeoman because Yeoman does have some issues on Windows computers, and getting it set up can be slightly challenging.

For those not using Yeoman, we will take a look at a sample application structure (which can be found in the *chapter3/sample-app* folder in our GitHub examples repository), which follows the recommended structure, as well as the structure generated by Yeoman. The files in the application can be broken into the following categories:

JS source files
> Take a look at the *app/scripts* folder. This is where all your JS source code lives. One main file (*app/scripts/app.js*) will set up the the Angular module and the routes for your application.
>
> In addition, there is a separate folder—*app/scripts/controller*—which houses the individual controllers. Controllers provide the action and publish data to the scope which will then be displayed in the view. Usually, they correspond one to one with the view.
>
> Directives, filters, and services can also be found under *app/scripts*, either as complete files (directives.js, filters.js, services.js), or individually, if they are nice and complex.

HTML Angular template files
> Now, every AngularJS partial template that Yeoman creates can be found in the *app/views* folder. This will mirror our *app/scripts/controller* folder for the most part.
>
> There is one other important Angular template file, which is the main *app/index.html*. This is responsible for sourcing the AngularJS source files, as well as any source files you create for your application.

If you end up creating a new JS file, ensure that you add it to the *index.html*, and also update the main module and the routes (Yeoman does this for you as well!).

JS library dependencies
> Yeoman provides you the *app/scripts/vendor* folder for all JS source dependencies. Want to use Underscore (*http://documentcloud.github.com/underscore/*) or SocketIO (*http://socket.io/*) in your application? No problem—add the dependency to the vendor folder (and your *index.html*!) and start referencing it in your application.

Static resources
> You are creating an HTML application in the end, and it is a given that you will have CSS and image dependencies that you need served as part of your application.

The *app/styles* and *app/img* folders are for this very purpose. Just add what you need and start referring to them (with the correct relative paths, of course!) in your application.

Yeoman does not create the *app/img* path by default.

Unit tests

Testing is super important, and totally effortless when it comes to AngularJS. The *test/spec* folder should mirror your *app/scripts* in terms of tests. Each file should have a mirror spec file which has its unit tests. The seed creates a stub for each controller file, under *test/spec/controllers*, with the same name as the original controller. These are Jasmine-style specs, which describe a specification for each expected behavior of the controller.

Integration tests

AngularJS comes with end-to-end testing support built right into the library. All your E2E tests, in the form of Jasmine specs, are saved under the folder *tests/e2e*.

Yeoman does not create the tests/folder by default.

While the E2E tests might look like Jasmine, they are not. They are functions that are executed asynchronously, in the future, by the Angular Scenario Runner. So don't expect to be able to do stuff like you would in a normal Jasmine test (like console.log on the value of a repeater).

There is also a simple HTML file generated that can be opened by itself in a browser to run the tests manually. Yeoman doesn't generate the stubs for these yet, but they follow a similar style to the unit tests.

Configuration files

There are two configuration files needed. The first one, *karma.conf.js*, is generated by Yeoman for you and is used to run the unit tests. The second one, which Yeoman does not generate yet, is the *karma.e2e.conf.js*. This is used to run the scenario tests. There is a sample file at the end of this chapter in the RequireJS integration section. The config details the dependencies and the files to use when running the unit tests using Karma. By default, it runs the Karma server at port 9876.

You might ask: how do I run my application? What about unit tests? How do I even write these various pieces that you are talking about?

Don't worry, young grasshopper, all in due time. In this chapter, we will deal with setting up your project and development environment so that things can move along at a rapid pace once we do start churning out some awesome code. What code you write, and how it hooks together to form your final awesome application, will come in the next few chapters.

Tools

AngularJS is just one part of your toolkit that allows you to actually develop your web pages. In this section, we will take a look at various tools that you would use to ensure efficient and fast development, from IDEs to test runners to debuggers.

IDEs

Let's start with how you actually edit your source code. There is a whole slew of JavaScript editors out there, both free and paid. Things have come a long way from the days when Emacs or Vi was the best option to develop in JS. Nowadays, IDEs come with syntax highlighting, auto-completion, and so much more, and it might be worth your while to give one a whirl. So which one should you use?

WebStorm. If you don't mind shelling out a few bucks (though there is a free 30-day trial!), then WebStorm by JetBrains (*http://www.jetbrains.com/webstorm/*) offers one of the most comprehensive web development platforms in recent times. It has features that were only previously available for typed languages, including code-completion (browser specific at that, as shown in Figure 3-1), code navigation, syntax, error highlighting, and out-of-the-box support for multiple libraries and frameworks. In addition, there is some very nice integration for debugging JavaScript right from the IDE while it is executing in Chrome.

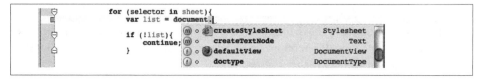

Figure 3-1. Browser specific code completion in WebStorm

The biggest reason you should seriously consider WebStorm for AngularJS development is that it is one of the only IDEs that has an AngularJS plug-in. The plug-in gives you auto-complete support for AngularJS HTML tags right in your HTML templates. In addition, one of the coolest things it supports is the concept of live templates. These are pre-formed templates for common code snippets that you would otherwise type from scratch every time. So instead of typing the following:

```
directive('$directiveName$', function factory($injectables$) {
  var directiveDefinitionObject = {
    $directiveAttrs$
    compile: function compile(tElement, tAttrs, transclude) {
      $END$
      return function (scope, element, attrs) {
      }
    }
  };
  return directiveDefinitionObject;
});
```

in WebStorm, you can just type:

```
ngdc
```

and press the *tab* key to get the same thing. This is just one of the many code-completions the plug-in provides.

Running Your Application

Now let's talk about how we get to the payload of all that we do—seeing your application live, in the browser. To really get a feel for how the application would work, we need to have a web server serving our HTML and JavaScript code. I will explore two ways: one very simple way of running your application with Yeoman, and another not so easy, but just as good, method without Yeoman.

With Yeoman

Yeoman makes it simple for you to start a web server and serve all your static and AngularJS-related files. Just execute the following command:

```
yeoman server
```

and it will start up a server and open your browser with the main page of your AngularJS application. It will even refresh the browser whenever you make changes to your source code. How cool is that?

Without Yeoman

Without Yeoman, you would need to configure a web server to serve all the files in your main directory. If you don't know an easy way to do that, or don't want to waste time creating your own web server, you can quickly write a simple web server using ExpressJS (as simple as npm install -g express to get it) in Node. It might look something like the following:

```
// available at chapter3/sample-app/web-server.js

var express = require("express"),
```

```
    app      = express(),
    port     = parseInt(process.env.PORT, 10) || 8080;

app.configure(function(){
  app.use(express.methodOverride());
  app.use(express.bodyParser());
  app.use(express.static(__dirname + '/'));
  app.use(app.router);
});

app.listen(port);
console.log('Now serving the app at http://localhost:' + port + '/app');
```

Once you have the file, you can run the file using Node, by executing the following command:

```
node web-server.js
```

and it will start up the server on port 8080 (or one of your own choosing).

Alternatively, with Python in the folder with your application you could run:

```
python -m SimpleHTTPServer
```

Whichever way you decide to proceed, once you have the server configured, up and running, navigate to the following:

```
http://localhost:[port-number]/app/index.html
```

in your browser to see the application you have just created. Do note that you will have to manually refresh your browser to see the changes, unlike with Yeoman.

Testing with AngularJS

We have said it before (even right in this chapter), and we will say it again: testing is essential, and AngularJS makes it simple to write the right kind of unit and integration tests. While AngularJS plays nicely with multiple test runners, we strongly believe that Karma (*https://github.com/vojtajina/karma/*) trumps most of them providing the most robust, solid, and insanely fast test runner for all your needs.

Karma

Karma's main reason for existence is to make your test-driven development (TDD) workflow simple, fast, and fun. It uses NodeJS (*http://www.nodejs.org*) and SocketIO (*http://www.socket.io*) (you don't need to know what they are, just assume that they are awesome, cool libraries) to allow running your code, and tests in multiple browsers at insanely fast speeds. Go find out more at *https://github.com/vojtajina/karma/*.

TDD: An Intro

Test-driven development, or TDD, is an AGILE methodology that flips the development lifecycle by ensuring that tests are written first, before the code is implemented, and that tests drive the development (and are not just used as a validation tool).

The tenets of TDD are simple:

- Code is written only when there is a failing test that requires the code to pass
- The bare minimum amount of code is written to ensure that the test passes
- Duplication is removed at every step
- Once all tests are passing, the next failing test is added for the next required functionality.

These simple rules ensure that:

- Your code develops organically, and that every line of code written is purposeful.
- Your code remains highly modular, cohesive, and reusable (as you need to be able to test it).
- You provide a comprehensive array of tests to prevent future breakages and bugs.
- The tests also act as specification, and thus documentation, for future needs and changes.

We at AngularJS have found this to be true, and the entire AngularJS codebase has been developed using TDD. For an uncompiled, dynamic language like JavaScript, we strongly believe that having a good set of unit tests will reduce headaches in the future!

So how do we get this awesomeness that is Karma? Well, first ensure that NodeJS (*http://www.nodejs.org*) is installed on your machine. This comes with NPM (Node Package Manager), which makes it easy to manage and install the thousands of libraries available for NodeJS.

Once you have NodeJS and NPM installed, installing Karma is as easy as running:

```
sudo npm install -g karma
```

There you go. You are ready to start Karmaing (I just made that up, please don't go about using it in real life) in three easy steps!

Getting your config file up

If you used Yeoman to create your app skeleton, then you already have a ready-made Karma config file waiting for you to use. If not, just go ahead and execute the following command from the base folder of your application directory:

```
karma init
```

in your terminal console, and it will generate a dummy config file (*karma.conf.js*) for you to edit to your liking, with some pretty standard defaults. You can use that.

Starting the Karma server

Just run the following command:

```
karma start [optionalPathToConfigFile]
```

This will start the Karma server on port 9876 (the default, which you can change by editing the *karma.conf.js* file from the previous step). While Karma should open up a browser and capture it automatically, it will print all the instructions needed to capture another browser in the console. If you are too lazy to do that, just go to *http://localhost:9876* in another browser or device, and you are good to start running tests in multiple browsers.

 While Karma can capture the usual browsers automatically, on start (Firefox, Chrome, IE, Opera, and even PhantomJS), it is not limited to just those browsers. Any device on which you can browse to a URL can possibly be a runner for Karma. So if you open up the browser of your iPhone or Android device and browse to *http://machinename:9876* (provided it is accessible!), you could potentially run your tests on mobile devices as well.

Running the tests

Execute the following command:

```
karma run
```

That's it. You should get your results printed right in the console where you ran the command. Easy, isn't it?

Unit Tests

AngularJS makes it easy to write your unit tests, and supports the Jasmine style of writing tests by default (as does Karma). Jasmine is what we call a behavior-driven development framework, which allows you to write specifications that denote how your code should behave. A sample test in Jasmine might look something like this.

```
describe("MyController:", function() {

  it("to work correctly", function() {
    var a = 12;
    var b = a;

    expect(a).toBe(b);
    expect(a).not.toBe(null);
  });
});
```

As you can see, it lends itself to a very readable format, as most of the code that could be read in plain English. It also provides a very diverse and powerful set of matchers (like the expect clauses), and of course has the xUnit (*http://en.wikipedia.org/wiki/ XUnit*) staples of setUp and tearDowns (functions that are executed before and after each individual test case).

AngularJS provides some nice mockups, as well as testing functions, to allow you to create services, controllers, and filters right in your unit tests, as well as mock out HttpRequests and the like. We will cover this in Chapter 5.

Karma can be integrated with your development workflow to make it easier, as well as to get faster feedback on the code you have written.

Integration with IDEs
> Karma does not have plug-ins (yet!) for all the latest and greatest IDEs, but you don't really need any. All you need to do is add a shortcut command to execute "karma start" and "karma run" from within your IDE. This can usually be done by adding a simple script to execute, or the actual shell command, depending on your choice of editor. You should see the results every time it finishes running, of course.

Running tests on every change
> This is utopia for many TDD developers: being able to run all their tests, every time they press save, within a few milliseconds, and get results back quickly. And this can be done with AngularJS + Karma pretty easily. Turns out, the Karma config file (remember the *karma.conf.js* file from before?) has an innocuous-looking flag named "**autoWatch**". Setting it to true tells Karma to run your tests every time the file it watches (which is your source and test code) changes. And if you do "karma start" from within your IDE, guess what? The results from the Karma run will be available right within your IDE. You won't even need to switch to console or terminal to figure out what broke!

End-to-End/Integration Tests

As applications grow (and they tend to, really fast, before you even realize it), testing whether they work as intended manually just doesn't cut it anymore. After all, every time you add a new feature, you have to not only verify that the new feature works, but also that your old features still work, and that there are no bugs or regressions. If you start adding multiple browsers, you can easily see how this can become a combinatorial explosion!

AngularJS tries to ease that by providing a Scenario Runner that simulates user interactions with your application.

The Scenario Runner allows you to describe your application in a Jasmine-like syntax. Just as with the unit tests before, we will have a series of describes (for the feature), and individual its (to describe each individual functionality of the feature). As always, you can have some common actions, to be performed before and after each spec (as we call a test).

A sample test that looks at an application that filters a list of results might look something like the following:

```
describe('Search Results', function() {
  beforeEach(function() {
    browser().navigateTo('http://localhost:8000/app/index.html');
  });
  it('should filter results', function() {
    input('searchBox').enter('jacksparrow');
    element(':button').click();
    expect(repeater('ul li').count()).toEqual(10);
    input('filterText').enter('Bees');
    expect(repeater('ul li').count()).toEqual(1);
  });
});
```

There are two ways of running these tests. Either way you run them, though, you must have a web server started that serves your application (refer to previous section for more information on how to do that). Once that is done, use one of the following methods:

1. **Automated**: Karma now supports running of Angular scenario tests. Create a Karma config file with the following changes:

   a. Add ANGULAR_SCENARIO & ANGULAR_SCENARIO_ADAPTER to the files section of the config.

   b. Add a proxies section that redirects requests to the server to the correct folder where your test files are located, for example:

   ```
   proxies = {'/': 'http://localhost:8000/test/e2e/'};
   ```

   c. Add a Karma root to ensure that Karma's source files don't interfere with your tests, like so:

   ```
   urlRoot = '/_karma_/';
   ```

   Then just remember to capture your Karma server by browsing to *http://localhost:9876/_karma_*, and you should be free to run your tests using Karma.

2. **Manual**: The manual method allows you to open a simple page from your web server and run (and see) all the tests. To do so, you must:

   a. Create a simple *runner.html* file, which sources the *angular-scenario.js* file from the Angular library.

   b. Source all your JS files which hold the specifications that you have written as part of your Scenario suite.

   c. Start your web server, and browse to the *runner.html* file.

Why should you use the Angular Scenario Runner over, say, an external third party integration or end-to-end test runner? There are some amazing benefits that you get from using the Scenario Runner, including:

AngularJS aware
The Angular Scenario Runner, as the name suggests, is made by and for Angular. Thus, it is AngularJS aware, and knows and understands the various AngularJS elements, like bindings. Need to input some text? Check the value of a binding? Verify the state of a repeater? All can be done easily through the use of the scenario runner.

No more random waits
The Angular awareness also means that Angular is aware of all XHRs being made to the server, and thus can avoid waiting for random intervals of time for pages to load. The Scenario Runner knows when a page has loaded, and thus is much more deterministic than a Selenium test, for example, where tests can fail by timing out while waiting for a page to load.

Debugging capabilities
Wouldn't it be nice if you could look at your code, dig into the JavaScript, and pause and resume the test when you wanted to, all while the Scenario tests were running? With the Angular Scenario Runner, all this is possible, and much more.

Compilation

Compilation in the JavaScript world usually means minification of the code, though there is some amount of actual compilation possible using the Google Closure Library. But why would you want to convert all that glorious, well-written, and easily understandable code to almost pure gibberish?

One reason is the goal of making applications that are quick and responsive for the user. That is a major reason why client-side applications took off like they did a few years ago. And the sooner you can get your application up and running, the sooner it will be responsive.

That responsiveness is the motivation of minification of JS code. The smaller the code, the smaller the payload, and the faster the transmission of the file to the user's browser. This becomes especially important in mobile apps, where size becomes the bottleneck.

There are a few ways you can minify the AngularJS code that you have written for your app, each with varying levels of effectiveness.

Basic and simple optimization

This involves minifying all the variables that you use in your code, but avoiding minifying the properties. This is known as the Simple optimization pass in Closure Compiler.

This will not give you a great reduction in file size, but you'll still get a substantial one, for minimal overhead.

The reason this works is that the compiler (Closure (*https://developers.google.com/closure/compiler/*) or UglifyJS (*https://github.com/mishoo/UglifyJS*)) avoids renaming properties that are referenced from the templates. Thus, your templates continue to work, and only local variables and parameters are renamed.

With Google Closure, this is as simple as calling:

```
java -jar closure_compiler.jar --compilation_level SIMPLE_OPTIMIZATIONS
                               --js path/to/file.js
```

Advanced optimization

Advanced optimization is a bit more tricky, as it tries to rename pretty much any and every function possible. To get this level of optimization to work, you will need to handhold the compiler a bit by telling it explicitly (through the use of an ex terns file) which functions, variables, and properties should not be renamed. These are generally the functions and properties accessed by the templates.

The compiler will use this `externs` file and then rename everything else. If done properly, this can result in a substantial reduction in the size of your JavaScript, but it does require a significant amount of work, including updating the `externs` file every time your code changes.

One thing to keep in mind: you have to use the declared form of dependency injection (specifying the `$inject` property on the controller) when you want to minify your code.

This will not work:

```
function MyController($scope, $resource) {
  // Stuff here
}
```

You will need to do one of the following instead:

```
function MyController($scope, $resource) {
  // Same stuff here
}

MyController.$inject = ['$scope', '$resource'];
```

or use the module, like so:

```
myAppModule.controller('MyController', ['$scope',
                                        '$resource',
                                        function($scope, $resource) {
  // Same stuff here
}]);
```

This is the only way AngularJS can figure out which service or variable you were originally asking for once all the variables are obfuscated or compressed.

 It is generally good practice to use the array-style injection all the time, to avoid bugs later when you start compiling the code. Scratching your head later and trying to figure out why the provider of the $e variable (the minified, obfuscated version of some service) is suddenly missing is just not worth it.

Other Awesome Tools

In this section, we will take a look at some other tools that will help ease your development flow and make you that much more productive. These range from debugging with Batarang to actual coding and development with Yeoman.

Debugging

When you work with JavaScript, debugging your code in the browser is going to become second nature. The sooner you accept that, the better off you will be. Thankfully, things have come a long way since the old days when there was no Firebug. Now, regardless of the choice of browser, there is generally something you can use to step in to your code, analyze your errors, and figure out the state of the application. Get to know the Developer Tools in Chrome and Internet Explorer; Firebug works across Firefox and Chrome.

A few further tips to help you out when debugging your application:

- Always, always switch to the non-minified version of all your source code and dependencies when you want to debug. Not only will you get better variable names, you'll also get line numbers and actual useful information and debugging capabilities.

- Try to keep your source code in individual JS files, not inlined in HTML.

- Breakpoints are useful! They allow you to check the state of your application, its models, and everything in between at a given point in time.
- "Pause on all exceptions" is a very useful option that is built in to most developer tools nowadays. The debugger will halt when an exception occurs, and highlight the line causing it.

Batarang

And then, of course, we have Batarang. Batarang is a Chrome extension that adds AngularJS knowledge to the built-in Developer Tools suite in Google Chrome. Once installed (you can get it from *http://bit.ly/batarangjs*), it adds another tab to the Developer Tools panel of Chrome called AngularJS.

Have you ever wondered what the current state of your AngularJS application is? What each model, each scope, and each variable currently contains? How is the performance of your application? if you haven't yet, trust me, you will! And when you do, Batarang is there for you!

There are four main useful additions in Batarang.

Model tab

Batarang allows you to dig into the scope, from the root downwards. You can then see how scopes are nested and how models are attached to them (as shown in Figure 3-2). You can even change them in real time and see the changes reflected in your application. How cool is that?

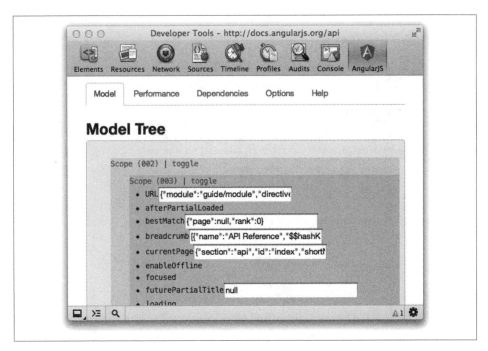

Figure 3-2. Model tree in Batarang

Performance tab

The performance tab must be enabled separately, as it injects some special JavaScript juice into your application. Once you enable it, you can look at various scopes and models, and evaluate the performance of all the watch expressions in each scope (as shown in Figure 3-3). The performance also gets updated as you use the app, so it works in real time as well!

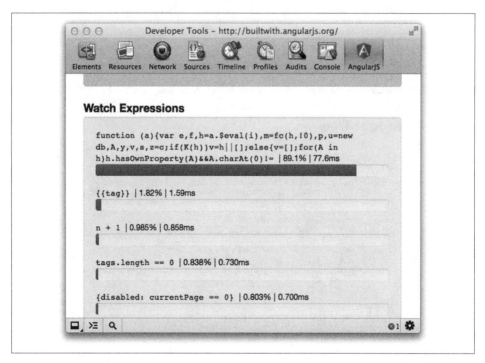

Figure 3-3. Performance tab in Batarang

Service dependencies

For a simple application, you won't have more than one or two dependencies for your controllers and services. But in a real, full-scale application, service dependency management can become nightmarish without the proper tool support. Batarang is there for you, filling this very hole, as it gives you a clean, simple way of visualizing your service dependency chart (as shown in Figure 3-4).

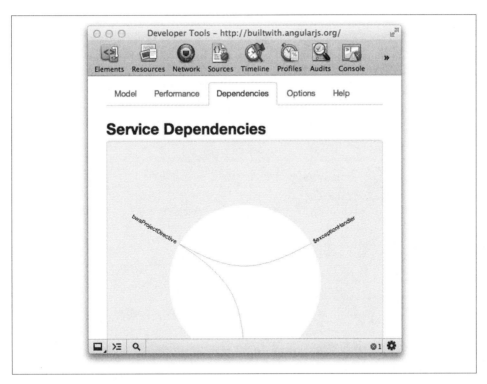

Figure 3-4. Charting dependencies in Batarang

Elements properties and console access

When you dig through the HTML template code of an AngularJS application, there is now an additional AngularJS Properties section in the Properties pane of the Elements tab. This allows you to inspect the models attached to a given element's scope. It also exposes the scope of the element to the console, so that you can access it through the $scope variable in the console. This is shown in Figure 3-5.

Figure 3-5. AngularJS properties within Batarang

Yeoman: Optimizing Your Workflow

There are quite a few tools that have sprung up to help optimize your workflow when developing web applications. Yeoman, which we touched upon in previous sections, is one such tool that boasts an impressive set of features, including:

- Lightning-fast scaffolding
- Built-in preview server
- Integrated package management
- An awesome build process
- Unit testing using PhantomJS

It also integrates nicely and extensively with AngularJS, which is one of the foremost reasons why we strongly recommend using it for any AngularJS project. Let's walk through the various ways that Yeoman makes your life easier:

Installing Yeoman

Installing Yeoman is quite an involved process, but there are scripts to help you through it.

On a Mac/Linux machine, run the following command:

```
curl -L get.yeoman.io | bash
```

and just follow the instructions it prints to get Yeoman.

For Windows, or if you run into any issues, go to *https://github.com/yeoman/yeoman/ wiki/Manual-Install* and follow the instructions there to get you unblocked.

Starting a Fresh AngularJS project

As previously mentioned, even a simple AngularJS project has quite a bit of seeding that needs to be done, from the templates, the basic controllers, and the library dependencies, to everything else that needs to be structured. You could do it yourself manually, or use Yeoman to do it for you.

Simply create a folder for your project (the name of the folder will be taken as the project name by Yeoman), and then run:

```
yeoman init angular
```

This will create the entire structure detailed in the Project Organization part of this chapter for you, including the skeletons for rendering your routes, your unit tests, and more.

Running Your Server

If you don't use Yeoman, you will have to create an HTTP server that serves your front-end code. But with Yeoman, you get a built-in server that is pre-configured and has some nice added benefits. You can start the server using:

```
yeoman server
```

This not only starts a web server that serves your code, but it also automatically opens your web browser and refreshes your browser when you make changes to your application.

Adding New Routes, Views, and Controllers

Adding a new route to Angular involves multiple steps, including:

- Sourcing the New Controller JS file in the *index.html*
- Adding the correct route to the AngularJS module

- Creating the template HTML
- Adding unit tests

All of this can be accomplished in a single step in Yeoman with the following command:

```
yeoman init angular:route routeName
```

So if you ended up running `yeoman init angular:route home`, it would:

- Create a *home.js* controller skeleton in the *app/scripts/controllers* folder
- Create a *home.js* test spec skeleton in the *test/specs/controllers* folder
- Add the *home.html* template to the *app/views* folder
- Hook up the home route in the main app module (*app/scripts/app.js* file)

All of this from a single command!

The Testing Story

We've already seen how ridiculously easy it is to start and run tests using Karma. In the end, just two commands were needed to run all your unit tests.

Yeoman makes it easier (if you can believe it). Anytime you generate a file using Yeoman, it also creates a testing stub for you to fill out. Once you've installed Karma, running tests with Yeoman is as simple as executing the following command:

```
yeoman test
```

Building Your Project

Building the production-ready version of your app can be a pain, or at least involve many steps. Yeoman alleviates some of this by allowing you to:

- Concatenate all your JS Scripts into one file
- Version your files
- Optimize images
- Generate Application Cache manifests

All these benefits come from just one command:

```
yeoman build
```

Yeoman does not support minification yet, but it is coming soon, according to the developers.

Integrating AngularJS with RequireJS

Getting your development environment just right is much easier if you get more done early. Modifying your development environment at a later stage will require modifications to a larger number of files. Dependency management and creating deployment packages are top worries for any sizable project.

With JavaScript, setting up your development environment used to be quite difficult, as it involved maintaining Ant builds, building scripts to concatenate your files, minifying them, and more. Thankfully, in the recent past, tools like RequireJS have emerged, which allow you to define and manage your JS dependencies, as well as hook them into a simpler build process. With these asynchronous load-management tools, which ensure that all dependencies are loaded before the code is executed, focusing on developing the actual features has never been easier.

Thankfully, AngularJS can and does play nice with RequireJS (*http://www.requir ejs.org*), so you can have the best of both worlds. For the purpose of this example, we will provide a sample setup that we have found to work nicely, and in a systematic, easy-to-follow way.

Let us take a look at the project organization (similar to the skeletons previously described, with minor changes):

1. **app**: This folder hosts all the app code that is displayed to the user. This includes HTML, JS, CSS, images, and dependent libraries.
   a. **/styles**: Contains all the CSS/LESS files
   b. **/images**: Contains images for our project
   c. **/scripts**: The main AngularJS codebase. This folder also includes our bootstrapping code, and the main integration with RequireJS
      i. **/controllers**: AngularJS controllers go here
      ii. **/directives**: AngularJS Directives go here
      iii. **/filters**: AngularJS filters go here
      iv. **/services**: AngularJS services go here
   d. **/vendor**: The libraries we depend on (Bootstrap, RequireJS, jQuery)
   e. **/views**: The HTML partials for the views and the components used in our project
2. **config**: Contains Karma configs for unit and scenario tests
3. **test**: Contains the unit and scenario (integration) tests for the app
   a. **/spec**: Contains the unit tests, mirroring the structure of the JS folder in the app directory

b. **/e2e**: Contains the end-to-end scenario specs

The first thing we need is the *main.js* file (in the app folder) that RequireJS loads, which then triggers loading of all the other dependencies. In this example, our JS project will depend on jQuery and Twitter Bootstrap in addition to our code.

```
// the app/scripts/main.js file, which defines our RequireJS config
require.config({
  paths: {
    angular: 'vendor/angular.min',
    jquery: 'vendor/jquery',
    domReady: 'vendor/require/domReady',
    twitter: 'vendor/bootstrap',
    angularResource: 'vendor/angular-resource.min',
  },
  shim: {
    'twitter/js/bootstrap': {
      deps: ['jquery/jquery']
    },
    angular: {
      deps: [ 'jquery/jquery',
              'twitter/js/bootstrap'],
      exports: 'angular'
    },
    angularResource: { deps:['angular'] }
  }
});

require([
    'app',
    // Note this is not Twitter Bootstrap
    // but our AngularJS bootstrap
    'bootstrap',
    'controllers/mainControllers',
    'services/searchServices',
    'directives/ngbkFocus'
    // Any individual controller, service, directive or filter file
    // that you add will need to be pulled in here.
    // This will have to be maintained by hand.
    ],
    function (angular, app) {
      'use strict';

      app.config(['$routeProvider',
        function($routeProvider) {
          // Define your Routes here
        }
      ]);
    }
);
```

We then define an *app.js* file. This defines our AngularJS app, and tells it that it depends on all the controllers, services, filters, and directives we define. We'll look at the files that are mentioned in the RequireJS dependency list in just a bit.

You can think of the RequireJS dependency list as a blocking import statement for JavaScript. That is, the function within the block will not execute until all the dependencies listed are satisfied or loaded.

Also notice that we don't individually tell RequireJS what directive, service, or filter to pull in, because that is not how this project is structured. There is one module each for controllers, services, filters, and directives, and thus it is sufficient to just define those as our dependencies.

```
// The app/scripts/app.js file, which defines our AngularJS app
define(['angular', 'angularResource', 'controllers/controllers',
        'services/services', 'filters/filters',
        'directives/directives'], function (angular) {
  return angular.module('MyApp', ['ngResource', 'controllers', 'services',
                                  'filters', 'directives']);
});
```

We also have a *bootstrap.js* file, which waits for the DOM to be ready (using RequireJS's plug-in, domReady), and then tells AngularJS to go forth and be awesome.

```
// The app/scripts/bootstrap.js file which tells AngularJS
// to go ahead and bootstrap when the DOM is loaded
define(['angular', 'domReady'], function(angular, domReady) {
    domReady(function() {
        angular.bootstrap(document, ['MyApp']);
    });
});
```

There is another advantage to splitting the bootstrap from the app, which is that we could potentially replace our mainApp with a fake or a mockApp for the purpose of testing. For example, if the servers you depend on are flaky, you could just create a fakeApp that replaces all $http requests with fake data to allow you to develop in peace. That way, you can just slip in a fakeBootstrap and a fakeApp into your application.

Now, your main *index.html* (which is in the app folder) could look something like:

```
<!DOCTYPE html>
<html> <!-- Do not add ng-app here as we bootstrap AngularJS manually-->
<head>
    <title>My AngularJS App</title>
    <meta charset="utf-8" />

    <link rel="stylesheet" type="text/css"
          href="styles/bootstrap.min.css">
    <link rel="stylesheet" type="text/css"
          href="styles/bootstrap-responsive.min.css">
```

```
    <link rel="stylesheet" type="text/css" href="styles/app.css">

</head>
<body class="home-page" ng-controller="RootController">
    <div ng-view ></div>

    <script data-main="scripts/main"
            src="lib/require/require.min.js"></script>
</body>
</html>
```

Now, we'll take a look at the *js/controllers/controllers.js* file, which will look almost exactly the same as *js/directives/directives.js*, *js/filters/filters.js*, and *js/services/services.js*:

```
define(['angular'], function(angular) {
    'use strict';
    return angular.module('controllers', []);
});
```

Because of the way we have our RequireJS dependencies structured, all these are guaranteed to run only after the Angular dependency has been satisfied and loaded.

Each of these files defines an AngularJS module, which will then be used by the individual controllers, directives, filters, and services to add on to the definition.

Let's take a look at a directive definition (such as our focus directive from Chapter 2):

```
// File: ngbkFocus.js

define(['directives/directives'], function(directives) {
  directives.directive(ngbkFocus, ['$rootScope', function($rootScope) {
    return {
      restrict: 'A',
      scope: true,
      link: function(scope, element, attrs) {
        element[0].focus();
      }
    };
  }]);
});
```

The directive itself is quite trivial, but let us take a closer look at what's happening. The RequireJS shim around the file says that my *ngbkFocus.js* depends on the module declaration file *directives/directives.js*. It then uses the injected directives module to add on its own directive declaration. You could choose to have multiple directives, or a single one per file. It is completely up to you.

One major note: if you have a controller that pulls in a service (say your RootControl ler depends on your UserService, and gets the UserService injected in), then you have to make sure that you define the file dependency to RequireJS as well, like so:

```
define(['controllers/controllers', 'services/userService'],
    function(controllers) {
  controllers.controller('RootController', ['$scope', 'UserService',
    function($scope, UserService) {
      // Do what's needed
  };
 }]);
});
```

That is basically how your entire source folder structure is set up.

But how does this affect my tests, you ask? We're glad you asked that question, because you are going to get the answer now!

The good news is that Karma does support RequireJS. Just install the latest and greatest version of Karma (using `npm install -g karma`).

Once you have done that, the Karma `config` for the unit tests also changes slightly. The following is how we would set up the unit tests to run for the project structure we have previously defined:

```
// This file is config/karma.conf.js.
// Base path, that will be used to resolve files
// (in this case is the root of the project)
basePath = '../';

// list files/patterns to load in the browser
files = [
    JASMINE,
    JASMINE_ADAPTER,
    REQUIRE,
    REQUIRE_ADAPTER,

    // !! Put all libs in RequireJS 'paths' config here (included: false).
    // All these files are files that are needed for the tests to run,
    // but Karma is being told explicitly to avoid loading them, as they
    // will be loaded by RequireJS when the main module is loaded.
    {pattern: 'app/scripts/vendor/**/*.js', included: false},

    // all the sources, tests  // !! all src and test modules (included: false)
    {pattern: 'app/scripts/**/*.js', included: false},
    {pattern: 'app/scripts/*.js', included: false},
    {pattern: 'test/spec/*.js', included: false},
    {pattern: 'test/spec/**/*.js', included: false},

    // !! test main require module last
    'test/spec/main.js'
];

// list of files to exclude
exclude = [];
```

```
// test results reporter to use
// possible values: dots || progress
reporter = 'progress';

// web server port
port = 8989;

// cli runner port
runnerPort = 9898;

// enable/disable colors in the output (reporters and logs)
colors = true;

// level of logging
logLevel = LOG_INFO;

// enable/disable watching file and executing tests whenever any file changes
autoWatch = true;

// Start these browsers, currently available:
// - Chrome
// - ChromeCanary
// - Firefox
// - Opera
// - Safari
// - PhantomJS
// - IE if you have a windows box
browsers = ['Chrome'];

// Continuous Integration mode
// if true, it captures browsers, runs tests, and exits
singleRun = false;
```

We use a slightly different format to define our dependencies (the `included: false` is quite important). We also add the dependency on REQUIRE_JS and its adapter. The final thing to get all this working is *main.js*, which triggers our tests.

```
// This file is test/spec/main.js

require.config({
    // !! Karma serves files from '/base'
    // (in this case, it is the root of the project /your-project/app/js)
    baseUrl: '/base/app/scripts',
    paths: {
        angular: 'vendor/angular/angular.min',
        jquery: 'vendor/jquery',
        domReady: 'vendor/require/domReady',
        twitter: 'vendor/bootstrap',
        angularMocks: 'vendor/angular-mocks',
        angularResource: 'vendor/angular-resource.min',
        unitTest: '../../../base/test/spec'
    },
```

```
    // example of using shim, to load non-AMD libraries
    // (such as Backbone, jQuery)
    shim: {
        angular: {
            exports: 'angular'
        },
        angularResource: { deps:['angular']},
        angularMocks: { deps:['angularResource']}
    }
});

// Start karma once the dom is ready.
require([
 'domReady',
 // Each individual test file will have to be added to this list to ensure
 // that it gets run. Again, this will have to be maintained manually.
 'unitTest/controllers/mainControllersSpec',
 'unitTest/directives/ngbkFocusSpec',
 'unitTest/services/userServiceSpec'
], function(domReady) {
domReady(function() {
    window.__karma__.start();
});
});
```

So with this setup, we can run the following:

```
karma start config/karma.conf.js
```

Then we can run the tests.

Of course there is a slight change when it comes to writing your unit tests. They need to be RequireJS-supported modules as well, so let's take a look at a sample test:

```
// This is test/spec/directives/ngbkFocus.js

define(['angularMocks', 'directives/directives', 'directives/ngbkFocus'],
    function() {
  describe('ngbkFocus Directive', function() {
    beforeEach(module('directives'));

    // These will be initialized before each spec (each it(), that is),
    // and reused
    var elem;
    beforeEach(inject(function($rootScope, $compile) {
      elem = $compile('<input type="text" ngbk-focus>')($rootScope);
    }));

    it('should have focus immediately', function() {
      expect(elem.hasClass('focus')).toBeTruthy();
    });
  });
});
```

Every test of ours will do the following:

1. Pull in `angularMocks`, which gets us `angular`, `angularResource`, and of course, `angularMocks`.

2. Pull in the high-level module (`directives` for directives, `controllers` for controllers, and so on), then the individual file it is actually testing (the `loadingIndicator`).

3. If your test depends on some other service or controller, make sure you also define the RequireJS dependency, in addition to telling AngularJS about it.

This kind of approach can be used with any test, and you should be good to go.

Thankfully, the RequireJS approach doesn't affect our end-to-end tests at all, so they can simply be done the way we have seen so far. A sample config follows, assuming that the server that runs your app is running on *http://localhost:8000*.

```
// base path, that will be used to resolve files
// (in this case is the root of the project
basePath = '../';

// list of files / patterns to load in the browser
files = [
  ANGULAR_SCENARIO,
  ANGULAR_SCENARIO_ADAPTER,
  'test/e2e/*.js'
];

// list of files to exclude
exclude = [];

// test results reporter to use
// possible values: dots || progress
reporter = 'progress';

// web server port
port = 8989;

// cli runner port
runnerPort = 9898;

// enable / disable colors in the output (reporters and logs)
colors = true;

// level of logging
logLevel = LOG_INFO;

// enable / disable watching file and executing tests whenever any file changes
autoWatch = true;

urlRoot = '/_karma_/';
```

```
proxies = {
 '/': 'http://localhost:8000/'
};

// Start these browsers, currently available:
browsers = ['Chrome'];

// Continuous Integration mode
// if true, it capture browsers, run tests and exit
singleRun = false;
```

Analyzing an AngularJS App

We talked about some of the commonly used features of AngularJS in Chapter 2, and then dived into how your development should be structured in Chapter 3. Rather than continuing with similarly deep dives into individual features, Chapter 4 will look at a small, real-life application. We will get a feel for how all the pieces that we have been talking about (with toy examples) actually come together to form a real, working application.

Rather than putting the entire application front and center, we will introduce one portion of it at a time, then talk about the interesting and relevant parts, slowly building up to the entire application by the end of this chapter.

The Application

GutHub is a simple recipe management application, which we designed both to store our super tasty recipes and to show off various pieces of an AngularJS application. The application:

- has a two-column layout.
- has a navigation bar on the left.
- allows you to create a new recipe.
- allows you to browse the list of existing recipes.

The main view is on the right, which gets changed—depending on the URL—to either the list of recipes, the details of a single recipe, or an editable form to add to or edit existing recipes. We can see a screenshot of the application in Figure 4-1.

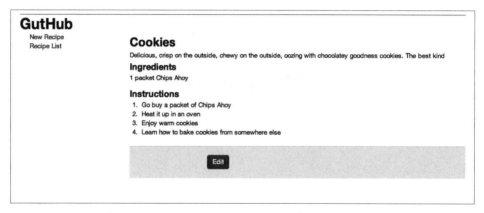

Figure 4-1. GutHub: A simple recipe management application

This entire application is available on our GitHub repo in *chapter4/guthub*.

Relationship Between Model, Controller, and Template

Before we dive into the application, let us spend a paragraph or two talking about how the three pieces of our application work together, and how to think about each of them.

The *model* is the truth. Just repeat that sentence a few times. Your entire application is driven off the model—what views are displayed, what to display in the views, what gets saved, everything! So spend some extra time thinking about your model, what the attributes of your object are going to be, and how you are going to retrieve it from the server and save it. The view will get updated automatically through the use of data bindings, so the focus should always be on the model.

The *controller* holds the business logic: how you retrieve your model, what kinds of operations you perform on it, what kind of information your view needs from the model, and how you transform the model to get what you want. The responsibility of validation, making server calls, bootstrapping your view with the right data, and mostly everything in between belongs on your controller.

Finally, the *template* represents how your model will be displayed, and how the user will interact with your application. It should mostly be restricted to the following:

- Displaying your model
- Defining the ways the user can interact with your application (clicks, input fields, and so on)

- Styling the app, and figuring out how and when some elements are displayed (show or hide, hover, and so on)
- Filtering and formatting your data (both input and output)

Realize that the template in Angular is not necessarily the view part of the Model View Controller design paradigm. Instead, the view is the compiled version of the template that gets executed. It is a combination of the template and the model.

What should not go into the template is any kind of business logic or behavior; this information should be restricted to the controller. Keeping the template simple allows a proper separation of concerns, and also ensures that you can get the most code under test using only unit tests. Templates will have to be tested with scenario tests.

But, you might ask, where does DOM manipulation go? DOM manipulation doesn't really go into the controllers or the template. It goes into AngularJS directives (but can sometimes be used via services, which house DOM manipulation to avoid duplication of code). We'll cover an example of that in our GutHub example as well.

Without further ado, let's dive right in.

The Model

We are going to keep the model dead simple for this application. There are recipes. They're about the only model object in this entire application. Everything else builds off of it.

Each recipe has the following properties:

- An ID if it is persisted to our server
- A name
- A short description
- Cooking instructions
- Whether it is a featured recipe or not
- An array of ingredients, each with an amount, a unit, and a name

That's it. Dead simple. Everything in the app is based around this simple model. Here's a sample recipe for you to devour (the same one referenced in Figure 4-1):

```
{
    "id": "1",
    "title": "Cookies",
    "description": "Delicious, crisp on the outside, chewy" +
        " on the outside, oozing with chocolatey goodness " +
        "cookies. The best kind",
    "ingredients": [
```

```
        {
          "amount": "1",
          "amountUnits": "packet",
          "ingredientName": "Chips Ahoy"
        }
      ],
      "instructions": "1. Go buy a packet of Chips Ahoy\n" +
          "2. Heat it up in an oven\n" +
          "3. Enjoy warm cookies\n" +
          "4. Learn how to bake cookies from somewhere else"
  }
```

We will go on to see how more complicated UI features can be built around this simple model.

Controllers, Directives, and Services, Oh My!

Now we finally get to sink our teeth into the meat of this delicious application. First, we will look at the directives and services code and talk a little bit about what it is doing, then we'll take a look at the multiple controllers needed for this application.

Services

```javascript
// This file is app/scripts/services/services.js

var services = angular.module('guthub.services', ['ngResource']);

services.factory('Recipe', ['$resource',
    function($resource) {
  return $resource('/recipes/:id', {id: '@id'});
}]);

services.factory('MultiRecipeLoader', ['Recipe', '$q',
    function(Recipe, $q) {
  return function() {
    var delay = $q.defer();
    Recipe.query(function(recipes) {
      delay.resolve(recipes);
    }, function() {
      delay.reject('Unable to fetch recipes');
    });
    return delay.promise;
  };
}]);

services.factory('RecipeLoader', ['Recipe', '$route', '$q',
    function(Recipe, $route, $q) {
  return function() {
    var delay = $q.defer();
    Recipe.get({id: $route.current.params.recipeId}, function(recipe) {
      delay.resolve(recipe);
```

```
    }, function() {
      delay.reject('Unable to fetch recipe ' + $route.current.params.recipeId);
    });
    return delay.promise;
  };
}]);
```

Let's take a look at our services first. We touched upon services in "Organizing Dependencies with Modules" on page 33. Here, we'll dig a little bit deeper.

In this file, we instantiate three AngularJS services.

There is a recipe service, which returns what we call an Angular Resource. These are RESTful resources, which point at a RESTful server. The Angular Resource encapsulates the lower level $http service, so that you can just deal with objects in your code.

With just that single line of code—return $resource—(and of course, a dependency on the guthub.services module), we can now put recipe as an argument in any of our controllers, and it will be injected into the controller. Furthermore, each recipe object has the following methods built in:

- Recipe.get()
- Recipe.save()
- Recipe.query()
- Recipe.remove()
- Recipe.delete()

 If you are going to use Recipe.delete, and want your application to work in IE, you will have to call it like so: Recipe[delete](). This is because delete is a keyword in IE.

Of the the previous methods, all but query work with a single recipe; query() returns an array of recipes by default.

The line of code that declares the resource—return $resource—also does a few more nice things for us:

1. Notice the :id in the URL specified for the RESTful resource. It basically says that when you make any query (say, Recipe.get()), if you pass in an object with an id field, then the value of that field will be added to the end of the URL.

   That is, calling Recipe.get({id: 15}) will make a call to /recipe/15.

2. What about that second object? The `{id: @id}`? Well, as they say, a line of code is worth a thousand explanations, so let's take a simple example.

Say we have a `recipe` object, which has the necessary information already stored within it, including an `id`.

Then, we can save it by simply doing the following:

```
// Assuming existingRecipeObj has all the necessary fields,
// including id (say 13)
var recipe = new Recipe(existingRecipeObj);
recipe.$save();
```

This will make a POST request to */recipe/13*.

The `@id` tells it to pick the `id` field from its object and use that as the `id` parameter. It's an added convenience that can save a few lines of code.

There are two other services in *apps/scripts/services/services.js*. Both of them are Loaders; one loads a single recipe (`RecipeLoader`), and the other loads all recipes (`MultiRecipeLoader`). These are used when we hook up our routes. At their cores, both of them behave very similarly. The flow of both these services is as follows:

1. Create a `$q` deferred object (these are AngularJS promises, used for chaining asynchronous functions).

2. Make a call to the server.

3. Resolve the deferred object when the server returns the value.

4. Return the promise that will be used by the routing mechanism of AngularJS.

Promises in an AngularJS land

A promise is an interface that deals with objects that are returned or get filled in at a future point in time (basically, asynchronous actions). At its core, a promise is an object with a `then()` function.

To showcase the advantages, let us take an example where we need to fetch the current profile of a user:

```
var currentProfile = null;
var username = 'something';

fetchServerConfig(function(serverConfig) {
  fetchUserProfiles(serverConfig.USER_PROFILES, username,
    function(profiles) {
    currentProfile = profiles.currentProfile;
  });
});
```

There are a few problems with this approach:

1. The resultant code is an indentation nightmare, especially if you have to chain multiple calls.

2. Errors reported in between callbacks and functions have a tendency to be lost, unless you handle them manually at each step.

3. You have to encapsulate the logic of what you want to do with `currentProfile` in the innermost callback, either directly, or through a separate function.

Promises solve these issues. Before we go into the how, let's take a look at the same problem implemented with promises:

```
var currentProfile =
  fetchServerConfig().then(function(serverConfig) {
  return fetchUserProfiles(serverConfig.USER_PROFILES, username);
}).then(function(profiles) {
  return profiles.currentProfile;
}, function(error) {
  // Handle errors in either fetchServerConfig or
  // fetchUserProfiles here
});
```

Notice the advantages:

1. You can chain function calls, so you don't get into an indentation nightmare.

2. You are assured that the previous function call is finished before the next function in the chain is called.

3. Each `then()` call takes two arguments (both functions). The first one is the success callback and the second one is the error handler.

4. In case of errors in the chain, the error will get propagated through to the rest of the error handlers. So any error in any of the callbacks can be handled in the end.

What about `resolve` and `reject`, you ask? Well, `deferred` in AngularJS is a way of creating promises. Calling `resolve` on it fulfills the promise (calls the success handler), while calling `reject` on it calls the error handler of the promise.

We'll come back to this again when we hook up our routes.

Directives

We can now move to the directives we will be using in our application. There will be two directives in the app:

`butterbar`

This directive will be shown and hidden when the routes change and while the page is still loading information. It will hook into the route-changing mechanism and automatically hide and show whatever is within its tag ,based on the state of the page.

`focus`

The `focus` directive is used to ensure that specific input fields (or elements) have the focus.

Let's look at the code:

```
// This file is app/scripts/directives/directives.js

var directives = angular.module('guthub.directives', []);

directives.directive('butterbar', ['$rootScope',
    function($rootScope) {
  return {
    link: function(scope, element, attrs) {
      element.addClass('hide');

      $rootScope.$on('$routeChangeStart', function() {
        element.removeClass('hide');
      });

      $rootScope.$on('$routeChangeSuccess', function() {
        element.addClass('hide');
      });
    }
  };
}]);

directives.directive('focus',
    function() {
  return {
    link: function(scope, element, attrs) {
      element[0].focus();
    }
  };
});
```

The preceding directive returns an object with a single property, `link`. We will dive deeper into how you can create your own directives in Chapter 6, but for now, all you need to know is the following:

1. Directives go through a two-step process. In the first step (the compile phase), all directives attached to a DOM element are found, and then processed. Any DOM manipulation also happens during the compile step. At the end of this phase, a linking function is produced.

2. In the second step, the link phase (the phase we used previously), the preceding DOM template produced is linked to the scope. Also, any watchers or listeners are added as needed, resulting in a live binding between the scope and the element. Thus, anything related to the scope happens in the linking phase.

So what's happening in our directive? Let's take a look, shall we?

The butterbar directive can be used as follows:

```
<div butterbar>My loading text...</div>
```

It basically hides the element right up front, then adds two watches on the root scope. Every time a route change begins, it shows the element (by changing its class), and every time the route has successfully finished changing, it hides the butterbar again.

Another interesting thing to note is how we inject the $rootScope into the directive. All directives directly hook into the AngularJS dependency injection system, so you can inject your services and whatever else you need into them.

The final thing of note is the API for working with the element. jQuery veterans will be glad to know that it follows a jQuery-like syntax (addClass, removeClass). AngularJS implements a subset of the calls of jQuery so that jQuery is an optional dependency for any AngularJS project. In case you do end up using the full jQuery library in your project, you should know that AngularJS uses that instead of the jQlite implementation it has built-in.

The second directive (focus) is much simpler. It just calls the focus() method on the current element. You can call it by adding the focus attribute on any input element, like so:

```
<input type="text" focus></input>
```

When the page loads, that element immediately gets the focus.

Controllers

With directives and services covered, we can finally get into the controllers, of which we have five. All these controllers are located in a single file (*app/scripts/controllers/controllers.js*), but we'll go over them one at a time. Let's go over the first controller, which is the List Controller, responsible for displaying the list of all recipes in the system.

```
app.controller('ListCtrl', ['$scope', 'recipes',
    function($scope, recipes) {
    $scope.recipes = recipes;
}]);
```

Notice one very important thing with the List Controller: in the constructor, it does no work of going to the server and fetching the recipes. Instead, it is handed a list of recipes already fetched. You might wonder how that's done. We'll answer that in the routing section of the chapter, but it has to do with the `MultiRecipeLoader` service we saw previously. Just keep that in the back of your mind.

With the List Controller under our belts, the other controllers are pretty similar in nature, but we will still cover them one by one to point out the interesting aspects:

```
app.controller('ViewCtrl', ['$scope', '$location', 'recipe',
    function($scope, $location, recipe) {
  $scope.recipe = recipe;

  $scope.edit = function() {
    $location.path('/edit/' + recipe.id);
  };
}]);
```

The interesting aspect about the View Controller is the edit function it exposes on the scope. Instead of showing and hiding fields or something similar, this controller relies on AngularJS to do the heavy lifting (as should you!). The `edit` function simply changes the URL to the edit equivalent for the recipe, and lo and behold, AngularJS does the rest. AngularJS recognizes that the URL has changed and loads the corresponding view (which is the same recipe in edit mode). Voila!

Next, let's take a look at the Edit Controller:

```
app.controller('EditCtrl', ['$scope', '$location', 'recipe',
    function($scope, $location, recipe) {
  $scope.recipe = recipe;

  $scope.save = function() {
    $scope.recipe.$save(function(recipe) {
      $location.path('/view/' + recipe.id);
    });
  };

  $scope.remove = function() {
    delete $scope.recipe;
    $location.path('/');
  };
}]);
```

What's new here are the `save` and `remove` methods that the Edit Controller exposes on the scope.

The `save` function on the scope does what you would expect it to. It saves the current recipe, and once it is done saving, redirects the user to the view screen with the same recipe. The `callback` function is useful in these scenarios to execute or perform some action once you are done.

There are two ways we could have saved the recipe here. One is to do it as shown in the code, by executing $scope.recipe.$save(). This is only possible because recipe is a resource object that was returned by the RecipeLoader in the first place.

Otherwise, the way you would save the recipe would be:

```
Recipe.save(recipe);
```

The remove function is also straightforward, in that it removes the recipe from the scope, and redirects users to the main landing page. Note that it doesn't actually remove it from our server, though it shouldn't be very hard to make that additional call.

Next, we have the New Controller:

```
app.controller('NewCtrl', ['$scope', '$location', 'Recipe',
    function($scope, $location, Recipe) {
  $scope.recipe = new Recipe({
    ingredients: [ {} ]
  });

  $scope.save = function() {
    $scope.recipe.$save(function(recipe) {
      $location.path('/view/' + recipe.id);
    });
  };
}]);
```

The New Controller is almost exactly the same as the Edit Controller. In fact, you could look at combining the two into a single controller as an exercise. The only major difference is that the New Controller creates a new recipe (which is a resource, so that it has the save function) as the first step. Everything else remains unchanged.

Finally, we have the Ingredients Controller. This is a special controller, but before we get into why or how, let's take a look:

```
app.controller('IngredientsCtrl', ['$scope', function($scope) {
  $scope.addIngredient = function() {
    var ingredients = $scope.recipe.ingredients;
    ingredients[ingredients.length] = {};
  };
  $scope.removeIngredient = function(index) {
    $scope.recipe.ingredients.splice(index, 1);
  };
}]);
```

All the other controllers that we saw so far are linked to particular views on the UI. But the Ingredients Controller is special. It's a child controller that is used on the edit pages to encapsulate certain functionality that is not needed at the higher level. The interesting thing to note is that since it is a child controller, it inherits the scope from the parent controller (the Edit/New controllers in this case). Thus, it has access to the $scope.recipe from the parent.

The controller itself does nothing too interesting or unique. It just adds a new ingredient to the array of ingredients present on the recipe, or removes a specific ingredient from the list of ingredients on the recipe.

With that, we finish the last of the controllers. The only JavaScript piece that remains is how the routing is set up:

```
// This file is app/scripts/controllers/controllers.js

var app = angular.module('guthub',
    ['guthub.directives', 'guthub.services']);

app.config(['$routeProvider', function($routeProvider) {
    $routeProvider.
      when('/', {
        controller: 'ListCtrl',
        resolve: {
          recipes: function(MultiRecipeLoader) {
            return MultiRecipeLoader();
          }
        },
        templateUrl:'/views/list.html'
      }).when('/edit/:recipeId', {
        controller: 'EditCtrl',
        resolve: {
          recipe: function(RecipeLoader) {
            return RecipeLoader();
          }
        },
        templateUrl:'/views/recipeForm.html'
      }).when('/view/:recipeId', {
        controller: 'ViewCtrl',
        resolve: {
          recipe: function(RecipeLoader) {
            return RecipeLoader();
          }
        },
        templateUrl:'/views/viewRecipe.html'
      }).when('/new', {
        controller: 'NewCtrl',
        templateUrl:'/views/recipeForm.html'
      }).otherwise({redirectTo:'/'});
}]);
```

As promised, we finally reached the point where the resolve functions are used. The previous piece of code sets up the Guthub AngularJS module, as well as the routes and templates involved in the application.

It hooks up the directives and the services that we created, and then specifies the various routes we will have in our application.

For each route, we specify the URL, the controller that backs it up, the template to load, and finally (optionally), a resolve object.

This resolve object tells AngularJS that each of these resolve keys needs to be satisfied before the route can be displayed to the user. For us, we want to load all the recipes, or an individual recipe, and make sure we have the server response before we display the page. So we tell the route provider that we have recipes (or a recipe), and then tell it how to fetch it.

This links back to the two services we defined in the first section, the MultiRecipeLoad er and the RecipeLoader. If the resolve function returns an AngularJS promise, then AngularJS is smart enough to wait for the promise to get resolved before it proceeds. That means that it will wait until the server responds.

The results are then passed into the constructor as arguments (with the names of the parameters being the object's fields).

Finally, the otherwise function denotes the default URL redirect that needs to happen when no routes are matched.

 You might notice that both the Edit and the New controller routes lead to the same template URL, *views/recipeForm.html*. What's happening here? We reused the edit template. Depending on which controller is associated, different elements are shown in the edit recipe template.

With this done, we can now move on to the templates, how these controllers hook up to them, and manage what is shown to the end user.

The Templates

Let us start by taking a look at the outermost, main template, which is the *index.html*. This is the base of our single-page application, and all the other views are loaded within the context of this template:

```
<!DOCTYPE html>
<html   lang="en" ng-app="guthub">
<head>
  <title>GutHub - Create and Share</title>
  <script src="scripts/vendor/angular.min.js"></script>
  <script src="scripts/vendor/angular-resource.min.js"></script>
  <script src="scripts/directives/directives.js"></script>
  <script src="scripts/services/services.js"></script>
  <script src="scripts/controllers/controllers.js"></script>
  <link href="styles/bootstrap.css" rel="stylesheet">
  <link href="styles/guthub.css" rel="stylesheet">
</head>
```

```
<body>
  <header>
    <h1>GutHub</h1>
  </header>

  <div butterbar>Loading...</div>

  <div class="container-fluid">
    <div class="row-fluid">
      <div class="span2">
        <!--Sidebar-->
        <div id="focus"><a href="/#/new">New Recipe</a></div>
        <div><a href="/#/">Recipe List</a></div>

      </div>
      <div class="span10">
        <div ng-view></div>
      </div>
    </div>
  </div>
</body>
</html>
```

There are five interesting elements to note in the preceding template, most of which you already encountered in Chapter 2. Let's go over them one by one:

ng-app

> We set the ng-app module to be GutHub. This is the same module name we gave in our angular.module function. This is how AngularJS knows to hook the two together.

script *tag*

> This is where AngularJS is loaded for the application. It has to be done before all your JS files that use AngularJS are loaded. Ideally, this should be done at the bottom of the body.

Butterbar

> Aha! Our first usage of a custom directive. When we defined our butterbar directive before, we wanted to use it on an element so that it would be shown when the routes were changing, and hidden on success. The highlighted element's text is shown (a very boring "Loading..." in this case) as needed.

Link href *Values*

> The hrefs link to the various pages of our single-page application. Notice how they use the # character to ensure that the page doesn't reload, and are relative to the current page. AngularJS watches the URL (as long as the page isn't reloaded), and works it magic (or actually, the very boring route management we defined as part of our routes) when needed.

`ng-view`
> This is where the last piece of magic happens. In our controllers section, we defined our routes. As part of that definition, we denoted the URL for each route, the controller associated with the route, and a template. When AngularJS detects a route change, it loads the template, attaches the controller to it, and replaces the `ng-view` with the contents of the template.

One thing that is conspicuous in its absence is the `ng-controller` tag. Most applications would have some sort of a `MainController` associated with the outer template. Its most common location would be on the body tag. In this case, we didn't use it, because the entire outer template has no AngularJS content that needs to refer to a `scope`.

Now let's look at the individual templates associated with each controller, starting with the "list of recipes" template:

```
<!-- File is chapter4/guthub/app/views/list.html -->
<h3>Recipe List</h3>
<ul class="recipes">
  <li ng-repeat="recipe in recipes">
    <div><a href="/#/view/{{recipe.id}}">{{recipe.title}}</a></div>
  </li>
</ul>
```

Really, it's a very boring template. There are only two points of interest here. The first one is a very standard usage of the `ng-repeat` tag. It picks up all the recipes from the `scope`, and repeats over them.

The second is the usage of the `ng-href` tag instead of `href`. This is purely to avoid having a bad link during the time that AngularJS is loading up. The `ng-href` ensures that at no time is a malformed link presented to the user. Always use this whenever your URLs are dynamic instead of static.

Of course you might wonder: where is the controller? There is no `ng-controller` defined, and there really was no Main Controller defined. This is where route mapping comes into play. If you remember (or peek back a few pages), the / route redirected to the list template and had the List Controller associated with it. Thus, when any references are made to variables and the like, it is within the scope of the List Controller.

Now we move on to something with a little bit more meat: the view form.

```
<!-- file is chapter4/guthub/app/views/viewRecipe.html -->
<h2>{{recipe.title}}</h2>

<div>{{recipe.description}}</div>

<h3>Ingredients</h3>
<ul class="unstyled">
  <li ng-repeat="ingredient in recipe.ingredients">
    <span>{{ingredient.amount}}</span>
```

```
      <span>{{ingredient.amountUnits}}</span>
      <span>{{ingredient.ingredientName}}</span>
    </li>
  </ul>

  <h3>Instructions</h3>
  <div>{{recipe.instructions}}</div>

  <form ng-submit="edit()" class="form-horizontal">
    <div class="form-actions">
      <button class="btn btn-primary">Edit</button>
    </div>
  </form>
```

Another nice, small, contained template. We'll draw your attention to three things, though not necessarily in the order they are shown!

The first is the pretty standard ng-repeat. The recipes are again in the scope of the View Controller, which is loaded by the resolve function before this page is displayed to the user. This ensures that the page is not in a broken, unloaded state when the user sees it.

The next interesting usage is that of ng-show and ng-class to style the template. The ng-show tag has been added to the <i> tag, which is used to display a starred icon. Now, the starred icon is shown only when the recipe is a featured recipe (as denoted by the recipe.featured boolean value). Ideally, to ensure proper spacing, you would have another empty spacer icon, with an ng-hide directive on it, with the exact same AngularJS expression as shown in the ng-show. That is a very common usage, to display one thing and hide another on a given condition.

The ng-class is used to add a class to the <h2> tag ("featured" in this case) when the recipe is a featured recipe. That adds some special highlighting to make the title stand out even more.

The final thing to note is the ng-submit directive on the form. The directive states that the edit() function on the scope is called in case the form is submitted. The form submission happens when any button without an explicit function attached (in this case, the Edit button) is clicked. Again, AngularJS is smart enough to figure out the scope that is being referred to (from the module, the route, and the controller) and call the right method at the right time.

Now we can move on to our final template (and possibly the most complicated one yet), the recipe form template.

```
<!-- file is chapter4/guthub/app/views/recipeForm.html -->
<h2>Edit Recipe</h2>
<form name="recipeForm" ng-submit="save()" class="form-horizontal">
  <div class="control-group">
    <label class="control-label" for="title">Title:</label>
    <div class="controls">
```

```
      <input ng-model="recipe.title" class="input-xlarge" id="title" focus>
    </div>
  </div>

  <div class="control-group">
    <label class="control-label" for="description">Description:</label>
    <div class="controls">
      <textarea ng-model="recipe.description"
                class="input-xlarge"
                id="description"></textarea>
    </div>
  </div>

  <div class="control-group">
    <label class="control-label" for="ingredients">Ingredients:</label>
    <div class="controls">
      <ul id="ingredients" class="unstyled" ng-controller="IngredientsCtrl">
        <li ng-repeat="ingredient in recipe.ingredients">
          <input ng-model="ingredient.amount" class="input-mini">
          <input ng-model="ingredient.amountUnits" class="input-small">
          <input ng-model="ingredient.ingredientName">
          <button type="button"
                  class="btn btn-mini"
                  ng-click="removeIngredient($index)">
          <i class="icon-minus-sign"></i> Delete </button>
        </li>
        <button type="button"
                class="btn btn-mini"
                ng-click="addIngredient()">
          <i class="icon-plus-sign"></i> Add </button>
      </ul>
    </div>
  </div>

  <div class="control-group">
    <label class="control-label" for="instructions">Instructions:</label>
    <div class="controls">
      <textarea ng-model="recipe.instructions"
                class="input-xxlarge"
                id="instructions"></textarea>
    </div>
  </div>

  <div class="form-actions">
    <button class="btn btn-primary">Save</button>
    <button type="button"
            ng-click="remove()"
            ng-show="!recipe.id"
            class="btn">Delete</button>
  </div>
</form>
```

Don't panic. It looks like a lot of code, and it is a lot of code, but if you actually dig into it, it's not very complicated. In fact, a lot of it is simple, repetitive boilerplate to show editable input fields for editing recipes:

- The focus directive is added on the very first input field (the title input field). This ensures that when the user navigates to this page, the title field has focus so the user can immediately start typing in the title.

- The ng-submit directive is used very similarly to the previous example, so we won't dive into it much, other than to say that it saves the state of the recipe and signals the end of the editing process. It hooks up to the save() function in the Edit Controller.

- The ng-model directive is used to bind the various input boxes and text areas on the field to the model.

- One of the more interesting aspects on this page, and one we recommend you spend some time trying to understand, is the ng-controller tag on the ingredients list portion. Let's take a minute to understand what is happening here.

  We see a list of ingredients being displayed, and the container tag is associated with an ng-controller. That means that the whole <ul> tag is scoped to the Ingredients Controller. But what about the actual controller of this template, the Edit Controller? As it turns out, the Ingredients Controller is created as a child controller of the Edit Controller, thereby inheriting the scope of Edit Controller. That is why it has access to the recipe object from the Edit Controller.

  In addition, it adds the addIngredient() method, which is used by the highlighted ng-click, which is accessible only within the scope of the <ul> tag. Why would you want to do this? This is the best way to separate your concerns. Why should the Edit Controller have an addIngredients() method, when 99% of the template doesn't care about it? Child and nested controllers are awesome for such precise, contained tasks, and allow you to separate your business logic into more manageable chunks.

- The other directive that we want to cover in some depth here is the form validation controls. It is easy enough in the AngularJS world to set a particular form field "as required." Simply add the required tag to the input (as is the case in the preceding code). But now what do you do with it?

  For that, we jump down to the Save button. Notice the ng-disabled directive on it, which says recipeForm.$invalid. The recipeForm is the name of the form which we have declared. AngularJS adds some special variables to it ($valid and $invalid being just two) that allow you to control the form elements. AngularJS looks at all the required elements and updates these special variables accordingly.

So if our Recipe Title is empty, `recipeForm.$invalid` gets set to true (and `$val id` to false), and our Save button is instantly disabled.

We can also set the max and min length of an input, as well as a Regex pattern against which an input field will be validated. Furthermore, there are advanced usages that can be applied to show certain error messages only when specific conditions are met. Let us diverge for a bit with a small example:

```
<form name="myForm">
User name: <input type="text"
                  name="userName"
                  ng-model="user.name"
                  ng-minlength="3">
<span class="error"
      ng-show="myForm.userName.$error.minlength">Too Short!</span>
</form>
```

In the preceding example, we add a requirement that the username be at least three characters (through the use of the `ng-minlength` directive). Now, the form gets populated with each named input in its scope—we have only `userName` in this example—each of which will have an `$error` object (which will further include what kind of error it has or doesn't have: `required`, `minlength`, `maxlength`, or `pattern`) and a `$valid` tag to signal whether the input itself is valid or not.

We can use this to selectively show error messages to the user, depending on the type of input error he is making, as we do in the previous example.

Jumping back to our original template—Recipe form template—there is another nice usage of the `ng-show` highlighted within the ingredients repeater `scope`. The Add Ingredient button is shown only beside the last ingredient. This is accomplished by calling an `ng-show` and using the special `$last` variable that is accessible inside a `repeater element scope`.

Finally, we have the last `ng-click`, which is attached to the second button, used for deleting the recipe. Notice how the button only shows if the recipe is not saved yet. While usually it would make more sense to write `ng-hide="recipe.id"`, sometimes it makes more semantic sense to say `ng-show="!recipe.id"`. That is, show if the recipe doesn't have an id, rather than hide if the recipe has an id.

The Tests

We have been holding off on showing you the tests that go along with the controller, but you knew they were coming, didn't you? In this section, we'll go over what kinds of tests you would write for which parts of the code, and how you would actually write them.

Unit Tests

The first and most important kind of test is the unit test. This tests that the controllers (and directives, and services) that you have developed are correctly structured and written, and that they do what you would expect them to.

Before we dive into the individual unit tests, let us take a look at the test harness that surrounds all of our controller unit tests:

```
describe('Controllers', function() {
  var $scope, ctrl;
  //you need to indicate your module in a test
  beforeEach(module('guthub'));
  beforeEach(function() {
    this.addMatchers({
      toEqualData: function(expected) {
        return angular.equals(this.actual, expected);
      }
    });
  });

  describe('ListCtrl', function() {....});
  // Other controller describes here as well

});
```

The harness (we are still using Jasmine to write these tests in a behavioral manner) does a few things:

1. Creates a globally (at least for the purpose of this test spec) accessible scope and controller, so we don't worry about creating a new variable for each controller.

2. Initializes the module that our app uses (GutHub in this case).

3. Adds a special matcher that we call equalData. This basically allows us to perform assertions on resource objects (like recipes) that are returned through the $re source service or RESTful calls.

> Remember to add the special matcher called equalData any time we want to do assertions on ngResource returned objects. This is because ngResource returned objects have additional methods on them that will fail normal expect equal calls.

With that harness in place, let's take a look at the unit tests for the List Controller:

```
describe('ListCtrl', function() {
  var mockBackend, recipe;
  // _$httpBackend_ is the same as $httpBackend. Only written this way to
```

```
    // differentiate between injected variables and local variables
    beforeEach(inject(function($rootScope, $controller, _$httpBackend_, Recipe) {
      recipe = Recipe;
      mockBackend = _$httpBackend_;
      $scope = $rootScope.$new();
      ctrl = $controller('ListCtrl', {
        $scope: $scope,
        recipes: [1, 2, 3]
      });
    }));

    it('should have list of recipes', function() {
      expect($scope.recipes).toEqual([1, 2, 3]);
    });
  });
```

Remember that the List Controller is one of the simplest controllers we have. The constructor of the controller just takes in a list of recipes and saves it to the scope. You could write a test for it, but it seems kind of silly (we still did it, because tests are awesome!).

Instead, the more interesting aspect is the MultiRecipeLoader service. This is responsible for fetching the list of recipes from the server and passing it in as an argument (when hooked up correctly via the $route service):

```
describe('MultiRecipeLoader', function() {
  var mockBackend, recipe, loader;
  // _$httpBackend_ is the same as $httpBackend. Only written this way to
  // differentiate between injected variables and local variables.
  beforeEach(inject(function(_$httpBackend_, Recipe, MultiRecipeLoader) {
    recipe = Recipe;
    mockBackend = _$httpBackend_;
    loader = MultiRecipeLoader;
  }));

  it('should load list of recipes', function() {
    mockBackend.expectGET('/recipes').respond([{id: 1}, {id: 2}]);

    var recipes;

    var promise = loader();
    promise.then(function(rec) {
      recipes = rec;
    });

    expect(recipes).toBeUndefined();

    mockBackend.flush();

    expect(recipes).toEqualData([{id: 1}, {id: 2}]);
  });
});
// Other controller describes here as well
```

We test the MultiRecipeLoader by hooking up a mock HttpBackend in our test. This comes from the *angular-mocks.js* file that is included when these tests are run. Just injecting it into your beforeEach method is enough for you to start setting expectations on it. In our second, more meaningful test, we set an expectation for a server GET call to *recipes*, which will return a simple array of objects. We then use our new custom matcher to ensure that this is exactly what was returned. Note the call to flush() on the mock backend, which tells the mock backend to now return response from the server. You can use this mechanism to test control flow and see how your application handles before and after the server returns a response.

We will skip View Controller, as it is almost exactly like the List Controller except for the addition of an edit() method on the scope. This is pretty simple to test, as you can inject the $location into your test and check its value.

Let us now jump to the Edit Controller, which has two points of interest that we should be unit testing. The resolve function is similar to the one we saw before, and can be tested the same way. Instead, we now want to see how we can test the save() and the remove() methods. Let's take a look at the tests for those (assuming our harnesses from the previous example):

```
describe('EditController', function() {
  var mockBackend, location;
  beforeEach(inject(function($rootScope,
                             $controller,
                             _$httpBackend_,
                             $location,
                             Recipe) {
    mockBackend = _$httpBackend_;
    location = $location;
    $scope = $rootScope.$new();

    ctrl = $controller('EditCtrl', {
      $scope: $scope,
      $location: $location,
      recipe: new Recipe({id: 1, title: 'Recipe'})
    });
  }));

  it('should save the recipe', function() {
    mockBackend.expectPOST('/recipes/1',
                           {id: 1, title: 'Recipe'}).respond({id: 2});

    // Set it to something else to ensure it is changed during the test
    location.path('test');

    $scope.save();
    expect(location.path()).toEqual('/test');

    mockBackend.flush();
```

```
    expect(location.path()).toEqual('/view/2');
  });

  it('should remove the recipe', function() {
    expect($scope.recipe).toBeTruthy();
    location.path('test');

    $scope.remove();

    expect($scope.recipe).toBeUndefined();
    expect(location.path()).toEqual('/');
  });
});
```

In the first test, we test the save() function. In particular, we ensure that saving first makes a POST request to the server with our object, and then, once the server responds, the location is changed to the newly persisted object's view recipe page.

The second test is even simpler. We simply check to ensure that calling remove() on the scope removes the current recipe, then redirects the user to the main landing page. This can be easily done by injecting the $location service into our test, and working with it.

The rest of the unit tests for the controllers follow very similar patterns, so we can skip over them. At their base, such unit tests rely on a few things:

- Ensuring that the controller (or more likely, the scope) reaches the correct state at the end of the initialization
- Confirming that the correct server calls are made, and that the right state is achieved by the scope during the server call and after it is completed (by using our mocked out backend in the unit tests)
- Leveraging the AngularJS dependency injection framework to get a handle on the elements and objects that the controller works with to ensure that the controller is getting set to the correct state

Scenario Tests

Once we are happy with our unit tests, we might be tempted to just lean back, smoke a cigar, and call it a day. But the work of an AngularJS developer isn't done until he has run his scenario tests. While unit tests assure us that every small piece of JS code is working as intended, we also want to ensure that the template loads, that it is hooked up correctly to the controllers, and that clicking around in the template does the right thing.

This is exactly what a scenario test in AngularJS does for you. It allows you to:

- Load your application
- Browse to a certain page
- Click around and enter text willy-nilly
- Ensure that the right things happen

So how would a scenario test for our "list of recipes" page work? Well, first of all, before we get started on the actual test, we need to do some groundwork.

For the scenario test to work, we will need a working web server that is ready to accept requests from the GutHub application, and will allow storing and getting a list of recipes from it. Feel free to change the code to use an in-memory list of recipes (removing the recipe $resource and changing it to just a JSON object dump), or to reuse and modify the web server we showed you in the previous chapter, or to use Yeoman!

Once we have a server up and running, and serving our application, we can then write and run the following test:

```
describe('GutHub App', function() {
  it('should show a list of recipes', function() {
    browser().navigateTo('/index.html');
    // Our Default GutHub recipes list has two recipes
    expect(repeater('.recipes li').count()).toEqual(2);
  });
});
```

CHAPTER 5

Communicating with Servers

Up to this point, we have mostly seen how your AngularJS application should be laid out, how the different AngularJS pieces fit together and work, and a bit on how templating in AngularJS works. Together, this allows you to build some sleek, sexy apps, but they are restricted mostly to the client side. We saw a little bit of the server-side communication with the $http service back in Chapter 2, but in this chapter, we'll dig a little bit deeper into how you would use it in a real-world application.

In this chapter, we will talk about how AngularJS allows you to communicate with your server, both at the lowest levels of abstraction and with the nice wrappers that it provides. Furthermore, we will go into how AngularJS can help you speed up your application with its built-in caching mechanism. If you want to develop a realtime application with AngularJS using SocketIO (*http://www.socket.io*), there is an example in Chapter 8 of a possible way to wrap SocketIO as a directive and use it, so we won't cover that here.

Communicating Over $http

The traditional way of making a request to the server from AJAX applications (using XMLHttpRequests) involves getting a handle on the XMLHttpRequest object, making the request, reading the response, checking the error codes, and finally processing the server response. It goes something like this:

```
var xmlhttp = new XMLHttpRequest();

xmlhttp.onreadystatechange = function() {
 if (xmlhttp.readystate == 4 && xmlhttp.status == 200) {
   var response = xmlhttp.responseText;
 } else if (xmlhttp.status == 400) { // or really anything in the 4 series
   // Handle error gracefully
 }
};
```

```
// Setup connection
xmlhttp.open("GET", "http://myserver/api", true);

// Make the request
xmlhttp.send();
```

This is a lot of work for such a simple, common, and often repeated task. If you want to do it repeatedly, you will likely end up creating wrappers or using a library.

The AngularJS XHR API follows what is commonly known as the Promise interface. As XHRs are asynchronous method calls, the response from the server will come back at an unknown future date and time (hopefully almost immediately!). The Promise interface guarantees how such responses will be dealt with, and allows consumers of the Promise to use them in a predictable manner.

Suppose we wanted to fetch a user's information from our server. If the API is available at */api/user*, and accepts the id as a URL parameter, then our XHR request using Angular's core $http service would look something like the following:

```
$http.get('api/user', {params: {id: '5'}
}).success(function(data, status, headers, config) {
 // Do something successful.
}).error(function(data, status, headers, config) {
 // Handle the error
});
```

If you are from the jQuery world, you should notice how similarly AngularJS and jQuery interact with asynchronous requests.

The $http.get method we used in the preceding example is just one of the many convenience methods that the core $http AngularJS service provides. Similarly, if you wanted to make a POST request using AngularJS with the same URL parameters and some POST data, you would do so as follows:

```
var postData = {text: 'long blob of text'};
 // The next line gets appended to the URL as params
 // so it would become a post request to /api/user?id=5
 var config = {params: {id: '5'}};
 $http.post('api/user', postData, config
).success(function(data, status, headers, config) {
 // Do something successful
}).error(function(data, status, headers, config) {
 // Handle the error
});
```

Similar convenience methods are provided for most of the common request types, including:

- GET
- HEAD
- POST
- DELETE
- PUT
- JSONP

Configuring Your Request Further

At times, the standard request options provided out of the box are not enough. This could be because you want to:

- Add some authorization headers for your request
- Change how caching is handled for the request
- Transform the request going out, or the response coming in, in certain set ways

In such cases, you can configure your request further through the optional configuration object passed to the requests. In the prior example, we used the config object to specify optional URL parameters. But even the GET and POST methods we showed there are convenience methods. The barebones method call would look something like:

```
$http(config)
```

What follows is a basic pseudo-code template for calling this method:

```
$http({
  method: string,
  url: string,
  params: object,
  data: string or object,
  headers: object,
  transformRequest: function transform(data, headersGetter) or
                    an array of functions,
  transformResponse: function transform(data, headersGetter) or
                     an array of functions,
  cache: boolean or Cache object,
  timeout: number,
  withCredentials: boolean
});
```

The GET, POST, and other convenience methods set the method, so you don't need to. The config object gets passed in as the last argument to $http.get, $http.post, so you can still use it while using any of the convenience methods.

You can change the request being made by passing the config object set with the following keys:

method
> A string representing the HTTP request type, like GET, or POST

url
> A URL string representing the absolute or relative URL of the resource being requested

params
> An object (a map to be precise) of string-to strings, representing keys and values that will be translated to URL parameters. For example:

```
[{key1: 'value1', key2: 'value2'}]
```

> would be converted to:

```
?key1=value1&key2=value2
```

> after the URL. If we use an object, instead of a string or a number, for the value, the object will be converted to a JSON string.

data
> A string or an object that will be sent as the request message data

timeout
> The time in milliseconds to wait before the request is treated as timed out

There are a few more options that can be configured, which we will explore in more depth in the following sections.

Setting HTTP Headers

AngularJS has default headers which it applies to all outgoing requests, which include the following:

1. Accept: application/json, text/plain, **/**
2. X-Requested-With: XMLHttpRequest

If there are any special headers you want to set, there are two ways of doing so.

The first way, if you think you are going to apply these headers to each and every outgoing request, is to make your special header part of the default headers for AngularJS. These are set in the $httpProvider.defaults.headers configuration object. This step is usually done in the config part of setting up your app. So if you wanted to enable "DO NOT TRACK" for all your GET requests, while removing the Requested-With header for all your requests, you could simply do the following:

```
angular.module('MyApp',[]).
  config(function($httpProvider) {
    // Remove the default AngularJS X-Request-With header
    delete $httpProvider.default.headers.common['X-Requested-With'];
    // Set DO NOT TRACK for all Get requests
    $httpProvider.default.headers.get['DNT'] = '1';
  });
```

If you want to set the headers for only certain requests, but not as a default, then you can pass the header in as part of the config object to $http service. The same custom header can be passed to a GET request as part of the second parameter, which also takes your URL parameters:

```
$http.get('api/user', {
  // Set the Authorization header. In an actual app, you would get the auth
  // token from a service
  headers: {'Authorization': 'Basic Qzsda231231'},
  params: {id: 5}
}).success(function() { // Handle success });
```

For a full-fledged example of how to handle authorization within your application, turn to the Cheatsheets example in Chapter 8.

Caching Responses

AngularJS provides a simple caching system for your HTTP GET requests out of the box. It comes disabled for all requests by default, but to enable caching for your requests, all you need to do is:

```
$http.get('http://server/myapi', {
  cache: true
}).success(function() { // Handle success });
```

This enables the cache, and AngularJS stores the response from the server. The next time a request is made for the same URL, AngularJS returns the response from the cache. The cache is also smart, so even if you make multiple simultaneous requests for the same URL, only one request is made to the server and the response is used to fulfill all the requests.

However, this might be jarring from a usability standpoint, as a user would first see the old results, then the new results would suddenly show up. For example, a user might be about to click on an item, and it might change under him.

Note that the response (even if it is being served from the cache), is still asynchronous in nature. In other words, expect your code to behave as it did when it first made the request.

Transformations on Requests and Responses

AngularJS applies some basic transformations on all requests and responses made through its $http service. These include:

Request transformations
> If the data property of the requested config object contains an object, serialize it into JSON format.

Response transformations
> If an XSRF prefix is detected, strip it. If a JSON response is detected, deserialize it using a JSON parser.

If you don't want some of the transformations, or want to add your own, then you can pass in your functions as part of the config. These functions get the HTTP request/response body, as well as the headers, and respond with the serialized, modified version. Set these config functions using the transformRequest and transformResponse keys, which are configured using the $httpProvider service in the config function of the module.

When would we use these? Let us assume that we have a server which is more attuned to the jQuery way of doing things. It would expect our POST data to come in the form key1=val1&key2=val2 (that is, a string), instead of the JSON form of {key1: val1, key2: val2}. While we could make this change at every request, or add a transform Request call individually, for the purpose of this example, we are going to add a general transformRequest, so that for all outgoing calls, this transformation from JSON form to a string happens. Here's how we would do this:

```
var module = angular.module('myApp');

module.config(function ($httpProvider) {
    $httpProvider.defaults.transformRequest = function(data) {
        // We are using jQuery's param method to convert our
        // JSON data into the string form
        return $.param(data);
    };
});
```

Unit Testing

So far, we have seen how you can use the $http service and configure it in all the possible ways you might want to. But what about writing some unit tests to ensure that it actually works?

As we have mentioned repeatedly, AngularJS was designed with testing in mind, so of course it has a mocked backend that allows you to test whether the right requests are being made, and even to control how and when the response is handled, right from your unit test.

Let us explore how you would unit test a controller that makes a request to your server, fetches some data from it, and sets it on the scope to be displayed by the view in some particular format.

Our NamesListCtrl is a very simple controller that has one purpose for its existence: to hit our names API, then store all the names on the scope.

```
function NamesListCtrl($scope, $http) {
  $http.get('http://server/names', {params: {filter: 'none'}}).
    success(function(data) {
      $scope.names = data;
  });
}
```

How would we unit test this? In our unit test, we would like to ensure that:

- NamesListCtrl can find all its dependencies (and get them injected correctly).
- The controller makes the request to fetch the names from the server as soon as it loads.
- The controller correctly saves the response to the names variable on the scope.

While we could construct a controller in our test, and inject a scope and fake HTTP service into it, let us instead construct the test the same way AngularJS would in its production code. This is the recommended way, despite it looking a bit more complicated. Let's take a look:

```
describe('NamesListCtrl', function(){
  var scope, ctrl, mockBackend;

  // AngularJS is responsible for injecting these in tests
  beforeEach(inject(function(_$httpBackend_, $rootScope, $controller) {
    // This is a fake backend, so that you can control the requests
    // and responses from the server
    mockBackend = _$httpBackend_;

    // We set an expectation before creating our controller,
```

```
    // because this call will get triggered when the controller is created
    mockBackend.expectGET('http://server/names?filter=none').
        respond(['Brad', 'Shyam']);
    scope = $rootScope.$new();

    // Create a controller the same way AngularJS would in production
    ctrl = $controller(PhoneListCtrl, {$scope: scope});
}));

it('should fetch names from server on load', function() {
    // Initially, the request has not returned a response
    expect(scope.names).toBeUndefined();

    // Tell the fake backend to return responses to all current requests
    // that are in flight.
    mockBackend.flush();

    // Now names should be set on the scope
    expect(scope.names).toEqual(['Brad', 'Shyam']);
});
});
```

Working with RESTful Resources

The $http service provides a very low-level implementation that allows you to make XHR requests, but still gives you a lot of control and flexibility. But in a majority of cases, we deal with objects and object models that are encapsulated with certain properties and methods, like a person object (with his details), or a credit card object.

In such cases, wouldn't it be nice if we could create a JS object that understands and represents this object model? If we could just edit the properties of this object, say save or update, and the state would get persisted on the server?

The $resource allows for this very capability. AngularJS resources allow us to define object models, and in a descriptive manner, to specify:

- The server-side URL for the resource
- The types of parameters that are commonly seen for such requests
- Some additional methods (you automatically get get, save, query, remove, and delete for free) that encapsulate specific functionality and business logic for the object model (like charge() for a credit card)
- The expected types of responses (an array or an object)
- The headers

When Can You Use Angular Resources?

You should only use Angular resources if your server side behaves in a RESTful manner. For the case of a credit card, which we will be using as an example in this part of the chapter that entails:

1. A GET request to */user/123/card* returns a list of credit cards for User 123.
2. A GET request to */user/123/card/15* returns the credit card with ID 15 for User 123.
3. A POST request to */user/123/card* with credit card info in the POST data creates a new credit card for User 123.
4. A POST request to */user/123/card/15* with credit card info in the POST data updates the credit card for User 123 with ID 15.
5. A DELETE request to */user/123/card/15* deletes the credit card with ID 15 for User 123.

In addition to providing objects that allow you to query the server as per your requirements, $resource also allows you to work with the returned objects as if they were persisted data models, make changes, and ask them to be persisted.

The ngResource is a separate, optional module. To use it, you need to:

- Include the *angular-resource.js* in your script files that are sourced.
- Include ngResource in your module dependency declaration (such as, angular.mod ule('myModule', ['ngResource'])).
- Use inject $resource where needed.

Before we look at how we would use the ngResource method of creating a resource, let us take a look at what it would take to create something similar using the base $http service. For our credit card resource, we want to be able to get, query, and save credit cards, in addition to being able to "charge" a credit card.

Here's one possible implementation:

```
myAppModule.factory('CreditCard', ['$http', function($http) {
  var baseUrl = '/user/123/card';
  return {
    get: function(cardId) {
      return $http.get(baseUrl + '/' + cardId);
    },
    save: function(card) {
      var url = card.id ? baseUrl + '/' + card.id : baseUrl;
      return $http.post(url, card);
```

```
    },
    query: function() {
      return $http.get(baseUrl);
    },
    charge: function(card) {
      return $http.post(baseUrl + '/' + card.id, card, {params: {charge: true}});
    }
  };
}]);
```

Instead, you could easily create an Angular service that reflects your resource through-out the app as follows:

```
myAppModule.factory('CreditCard', ['$resource', function($resource) {
  return $resource('/user/:userId/card/:cardId',
      {userId: 123, cardId: '@id'},
      {charge: {method:'POST', params:{charge:true}, isArray:false});
}]);
```

Now, whenever we ask for a CreditCard from the AngularJS injector, we get an Angular resource, which by default gives us a few methods to start off with. Table 5-1 lists what the methods are, and how they behave, so you know how the server should be config-ured.

Table 5-1. A credit card resource

Resource Function	Method	URL	Expected Return
CreditCard.get({id: 11})	GET	/user/123/card/11	Single JSON
CreditCard.save({}, ccard)	POST	/user/123/card with post data "ccard"	Single JSON
CreditCard.save({id: 11}, ccard)	POST	/user/123/card/11 with post data "ccard"	Single JSON
CreditCard.query()	GET	/user/123/card	JSON Array
CreditCard.remove({id: 11})	DELETE	/user/123/card/11	Single JSON
CreditCard.delete({id: 11})	DELETE	/user/123/card/11	Single JSON

Let's take the example of a credit card, which should make things clearer.

```
// Let us assume that the CreditCard service is injected here

// We can retrieve a collection from the server which makes the request
// GET: /user/123/card
var cards = CreditCard.query();

// We can get a single card, and work with it from the callback as well
CreditCard.get({cardId: 456}, function(card) {
// each item is an instance of CreditCard
expect(card instanceof CreditCard).toEqual(true);
card.name = "J. Smith";
// non-GET methods are mapped onto the instances
card.$save();
```

```
// our custom method is mapped as well.
card.$charge({amount:9.99});
// Makes a POST: /user/123/card/456?amount=9.99&charge=true
// with data {id:456, number:'1234', name:'J. Smith'}
});
```

A lot of things happen in the preceding example, so we'll call out the important parts one by one:

The Declaration

Declaring your own $resource is as simple as calling the injected $resource function (you know how to inject things by now, right?) with the right parameters.

The $resource function takes one required argument—the URL at which the resource is available—and two optional arguments: default parameters and additional actions you want to configure on the resource.

Notice that the URL parameter is parametrized (the : denotes a parameter. The :user Id states that the userId parameter will replace the text there, and the :cardId will be replaced by the value of the cardId parameter). If the parameter is not passed, then it will be replaced by an empty string.

The second parameter takes care of the default parameters to be passed along with each request. In this case, we pass in the userId as a constant 123. The cardId parameter is more interesting. We say cardId is "@id." This denotes that if I am using a returned object from the server, and I call any method on it (such as $save), then the cardId field is to be picked from the id property on the object.

The third argument is other methods we would like to expose on our custom resource. We'll cover this in depth in the following section.

Custom Methods

The third argument to the $resource call is optional additional methods you want to expose on your resource.

In this case, we specify a method charge. This can be configured by passing in an object, with the key being the method name to be exposed. The configuration needs to specify the method type of the request (GET, POST, and so on), the parameters that need to be passed as part of that request (charge=true in this case), and if the returned result is an array or not (not, in this case). Once that is done, you are free to start calling Credit Card.charge() whenever you want (as long as the user has charged in real life, of course!).

No Callbacks! (Unless You Really Want Them)

The third thing to notice is the return type of the resource call. Take a look at the `CreditCard.query()` call again. You will see that instead of assigning the cards in a callback, we are directly assigning them to the card's variable. With an asynchronous server request, will that code even work?

You would be correct to worry about whether the code will work, but the code is actually correct and will work. What's happening here is that AngularJS assigned a reference (an object or an array, depending on the expected return type), which will get populated at some point in the future when the server requests returns. In the meantime, the object will remain empty.

Since the most common flow with AngularJS apps is to fetch data from the server, assign it to a variable, and display it in the template, this shortcut is nice. In your controller code, all you have to do is make the server-side call, assign the return value to the right scope variable, and let the template worry about rendering it when it returns.

This approach will not work for you if you have some business logic you want executed on the return value. In such a case, you will have to depend on the callback, which is used in the `CreditCard.get()` call.

Simplified Server-Side Operations

Regardless of whether you use the shortcut return type or the callback, there are some other points you should note about the returned object.

The return value is not a plain old JS object, but in fact a "resource" type object. This means that in addition to the value returned by the server, it has some additional behavior attached to it (the `$save()` and `$charge()` in this case). This allows you to perform server-side operations with ease, for example by fetching data, making some changes, and persisting the changes to the server (the most common behavior in any CRUD app).

Unit Test the ngResource

The `ngResource` is an encapsulation, and uses the `$http` core AngularJS at its base. Thus, you already know how to unit test it. Nothing really changes from the unit testing example we saw for `$http`. You only need to know the final request that is expected to be made by the resource, tell the fake `$http` service about it, and everything else should be exactly the same. Let's take a look at a test for our preceding code:

```
describe('Credit Card Resource', function(){
  var scope, ctrl, mockBackend;

  beforeEach(inject(function(_$httpBackend_, $rootScope, $controller) {
    mockBackend = _$httpBackend_;
```

```
    scope = $rootScope.$new();
    // Assume that CreditCard resource is used by the controller
    ctrl = $controller(CreditCardCtrl, {$scope: scope});
}));

it('should fetched list of credit cards', function() {
    // Set expectation for CreditCard.query() call
    mockBackend.expectGET('/user/123/card').
        respond([{id: '234', number: '11112222'}]);

    ctrl.fetchAllCards();

    // Initially, the request has not returned a response
    expect(scope.cards).toBeUndefined();

    // Tell the fake backend to return responses to all current requests
    // that are in flight.
    mockBackend.flush();

    // Now cards should be set on the scope
    expect(scope.cards).toEqualData([{id: '234', number: '11112222'}]);
});
});
```

This test should look extremely similar to the simple $http unit test, except for one minor difference. Notice how in our expectation, instead of using the simple "equals" method, we are using a special toEqualData call. This expectation is smart enough to ignore the additional methods that the ngResource adds to an object.

The $q and the Promise

So far, we have seen how AngularJS implements its asynchronous, deferred API. The Promise proposal is the basis for how AngularJS structures its API. At its base, the Promise proposal dictates the following for asynchronous requests:

- Async requests return a promise instead of a return value.
- The Promise has a then function, which takes two arguments, a function to handle the "resolved" or "success" event, and a function to handle the "rejected" or "failure" event. These functions are called with the result, or the reason for the rejection.
- It is guaranteed that one of the two callbacks will be called, as soon as the result is available.

While most deferred/Q implementations follow this kind of approach, AngularJS' implementation is special for the following reasons:

- The $q is AngularJS aware, and thus is integrated with the scope model. This allows for faster propagation of resolution and less flicker/updates in the UI

- AngularJS templates also recognize the $q promises, and thus they can be treated as the resultant value themselves instead of a promise, which will be notified of the result.

- A smaller footprint, as AngularJS implements only the basic, most important functionality needed for common async tasks.

You might ask the question: why would you want to do something so crazy? Let's take a look at a standard problem you might run into with asynchronous functions:

```
fetchUser(function(user) {
  fetchUserPermissions(user, function(permissions) {
    fetchUserListData(user, permissions, function(list) {
      // Do something with the list of data that you want to display
    });
  });
});
```

This is the dreaded pyramid of doom that people complain about when working with JavaScript. The asynchronous nature of returns competes with the synchronous needs of the program, leading to multiple nested functions, making it that much harder to keep track of the current context.

In addition, there is also the matter of error handling. What is the best way to handle errors? Do you do it in each step? That also gets messy.

To fix this, the Promise proposal offers the concept of then, which takes the functions to execute in case of a success, on one hand, and error on the other, each of which can also be chained. So the preceding example, with the Promise API (AngularJS' implementation, at least), could be flattened to:

```
var deferred = $q.defer();

var fetchUser = function() {
  // After async calls, call deferred.resolve with the response value
  deferred.resolve(user);

  // In case of error, call
  deferred.reject('Reason for failure');
}
// Similarly, fetchUserPermissions and fetchUserListData are handled

deferred.promise.then(fetchUser)
  .then(fetchUserPermissions)
  .then(fetchUserListData)
  .then(function(list) {
    // Do something with the list of data
  }, function(errorReason) {
```

```
    // Handle error in any of the steps here in a single stop
});
```

The whole pyramid is flattened nicely, and provides scope for chaining, as well as a single point of error handling. You can use the same code in your application for handling asynchronous calls by including the $q AngularJS service. This mechanism also allows us to do something very cool: response interception!

Response Interception

We have covered making calls to the server, handling responses, wrapping the responses nicely in abstractions, and dealing with asynchronous calls. But in any real world application, you would end up having to do some common operations for each server call you made, tasks such as error handling, authentication, and other security considerations like pruning the data.

With a solid understanding of the $q API, we can now set about doing all of the above using Response Interceptors. Response Interceptors allow you (as the name would suggest) to intercept responses before they make it to the application, and apply your transformations, error handling, and everything else, including the kitchen sink.

Let us take an example which intercepts the responses and does some minor data transformation.

```
// register the interceptor as a service
myModule.factory('myInterceptor', function($q, notifyService, errorLog) {
  return function(promise) {
    return promise.then(function(response) {
       // Do nothing
       return response;
    }, function(response) {
      // My notify service updates the UI with the error message
      notifyService(response);
      // Also log it in the console for debug purposes
      errorLog(response);
      return $q.reject(response);
    });
  }
});

// Ensure that the interceptor we created is part of the interceptor chain
$httpProvider.responseInterceptors.push('myInterceptor');
```

Security Considerations

Now, when working with web applications, security is a huge concern and should be kept at the top of one's mind. AngularJS does provide some assistance when it comes to two common attack vectors, which we will cover in the following sections.

JSON Vulnerability

There is a very subtle JSON vulnerability which is exposed when a GET request is made to retrieve JSON information as an array (especially if the information is sensitive and requires login credentials or authentication to access).

The vulnerability involves a malicious site which uses a `<SCRIPT>` tag to make a request for the same information. Because you are still logged in, the malicious site uses your credential to request the JSON information, and gets it.

You might wonder how, because that information is still on your client, and the server cannot get a handle on that information. And usually, JSON objects returned as a result of sourcing a script will cause an error, though arrays are an exception.

But here's where the vulnerability kicks in: in JavaScript, it is possible to rewrite or re-declare built-in objects. In this vulnerability, the array constructor gets redefined, and in this redefinition, the malicious website can get a handle on the data, and send it to its own server.

There are two ways to prevent this vulnerability: always ensure that sensitive information is sent by JSON as a response to POST requests only, and return an object, or an invalid JSON expression as your result, then have some client-side logic to convert it into the actual data.

AngularJS allows you to prevent this vulnerability in both of these ways. In your application, you can (and should!) choose to retrieve JSON information through POST requests only.

Furthermore, you can configure your server to prefix:

```
")]}',\n"
```

before all your JSON responses. Thus, a normal response of:

```
['one', 'two']
```

would be returned as:

```
)]}',
['one', 'two']
```

AngularJS will automatically strip this prefix and only then process the JSON.

XSRF

XSRF (Cross-Site Request Forgery) attacks usually have the following characteristics:

- They involve sites that rely on authentication or a user's identity.
- They exploit the fact that the user remains logged in and authenticated to the site with the vulnerability.

- They make spurious HTTP/XHR requests that have (often harmful) side effects.

Consider the following example of an XSRF attack:

- User A is logged into his bank account (*http://www.examplebank.com*)
- User B realizes this, and gets User A to visit User B's home page
- The home page has a specially crafted image link which triggers the XSRF attack

```
<img src="http://www.examplebank.com/xfer?from=UserA&amount=10000&to=UserB">
```

If User A's bank keeps the authentication information in a cookie, and it hasn't expired, then when User A opens User B's website, it would trigger an unauthorized transfer from User A to User B.

So how does AngularJS help prevent this? It provides a two-step mechanism to prevent XSRF vulnerabilities.

On the client side, when performing XHR requests, the $http service reads a token from a cookie called XSRF-TOKEN and sets it as an HTTP header X-XSRF-TOKEN. Since only your requests from your domain could have read and set the token, you can be assured that the XHR came from your domain.

This also requires a slight modification of your server code, so that it sets a readable session cookie called XSRF-TOKEN on the first HTTP GET request. Subsequent requests to the server can verify that the value in the HTTP header matches the XSRF token set in the first request. Of course the token must be unique to every user, and must be verifiable by the server (to prevent the JavaScript from making up its own tokens).

CHAPTER 6

Directives

With directives, you can extend HTML to add declarative syntax to do whatever you like. By doing so, you can replace generic <div>s and <span>s with elements and attributes that actually mean something specific to your application. The ones that come with Angular provide basic functionality, but you can create your own to do things specific to your application.

First we're going to go over the directives API and how it fits within the Angular startup and runtime lifecycles. From there, we'll use this knowledge to create several classes of directives. We'll finish the chapter with how to write unit tests for directives and how to make these run quickly.

But first, a few notes on the syntax for using directives.

Directives and HTML Validation

Throughout this book, we've used Angular's built-in directives with the ng-directive-name syntax. Examples include ng-repeat, ng-view, and ng-controller. Here, the *ng* portion is the namespace for Angular, and the part after the dash is the name for the directive.

While we prefer this syntax for ease of typing, it isn't valid in many HTML validation schemes. To support these, Angular lets you invoke any directive in several ways. The following syntaxes, laid out in Table 6-1, are all equivalent to allow for your preferred validator to work properly:

Table 6-1. HTML Validation Schemes

Validator	Format	Example
none	namespace-name	ng-repeat=*item in items*
XML	namespace:name	ng:repeat=*item in items*
HTML5	data-namespace-name	data-ng-repeat=*item in items*
xHTML	x-namespace-name	x-ng-repeat=*item in items*

Because you can use any of these, the Angular documentation (*http://docs.angularjs.org/ api/*) lists directives with a camel-case format, instead of any of these options. For example, ng-repeat is found under the title *ngRepeat*. As you'll see in a bit, you'll use this naming format when defining your own directives.

If you don't use an HTML validator (most folks don't), you'll be just fine using the namespace-directive syntax as you've seen in the examples so far.

API Overview

A basic pseudo-code template for creating any directive follows:

```
var myModule = angular.module(...);

myModule.directive('namespaceDirectiveName', function factory(injectables) {
  var directiveDefinitionObject = {
    restrict: string,
    priority: number,
    template: string,
    templateUrl: string,
    replace: bool,
    transclude: bool,
    scope: bool or object,
    controller: function controllerConstructor($scope,
                                               $element,
                                               $attrs,
                                               $transclude),
    require: string,
    link: function postLink(scope, iElement, iAttrs) { ... },
    compile: function compile(tElement, tAttrs, transclude) {
      return {
        pre: function preLink(scope, iElement, iAttrs, controller) { ... },
        post: function postLink(scope, iElement, iAttrs, controller) { ... }
      }
    }
  };
  return directiveDefinitionObject;
});
```

Some of the options are mutually exclusive, most of them are optional, and all of them have details that are worth explaining.

Table 6-2 provides an overview of when you'd use each of the options.

Table 6-2. Directive definition options

Property	Purpose
restrict	Declare how directive can be used in a template as an element, attribute, class, comment, or any combination.
priority	Set the order of execution in the template relative to other directives on the element.
template	Specify an inline template as a string. Not used if you're specifying your template as a URL.
templateUrl	Specify the template to be loaded by URL. This is not used if you've specified an inline template as a string.
replace	If true, replace the current element. If false or unspecified, append this directive to the current element.
transclude	Lets you move the original children of a directive to a location inside the new template.
scope	Create a new scope for this directive rather than inheriting the parent scope.
controller	Create a controller which publishes an API for communicating across directives.
require	Require that another directive be present for this directive to function correctly.
link	Programmatically modify resulting DOM element instances, add event listeners, and set up data binding.
compile	Programmatically modify the DOM template for features across copies of a directive, as when used in ng-repeat. Your compile function can also return link functions to modify the resulting element instances.

Let's dig into the details.

Naming Your Directive

You create a name for your directive with a module's directive function, as in the following:

```
myModule.directive('directiveName', function factory(injectables)
```

Though you can name your directives anything you like, the convention is to pick a prefix namespace that identifies your directives and prevents them from colliding with external directives that you might include in your project.

You certainly wouldn't want to name them with an ng- prefix, as that might collide with Angular's bundled directives. If you work at SuperDuper MegaCorp, you could choose super-, superduper-, or even superduper-megacorp-, though you might choose the first option just for ease of typing.

As previously noted, Angular uses a normalized naming scheme for directives and will make camel-cased directive names available in templates in the five different validator-friendly varieties. For example, if you've picked your prefix as super- and you're writing a date-picker component, you might name it *superDatePicker*. In templates, you could then use it as super-date-picker, super:date-picker, data-super-date-picker, or another variant.

The Directive Definition Object

As previously mentioned, most of the options in the directive definition are optional. In fact, there are no hard requirements and you can construct useful directives out of many subsets of the parameters. Let's take a walk through what the options do.

restrict

The `restrict` property lets you specify the declaration style for your directive—that is, whether it can be used as an element name, attribute, class, or comment. You can specify one or more declaration styles using a character to represent each of them from the set in Table 6-3:

Table 6-3. Options for directive declaration usage

Character	Declaration style	Example
E	element	<my-menu title=*Products*></my-menu>
A	attribute	<div my-menu=*Products*></my-menu>
C	class	<div class=*my-menu:Products*></div>
M	comment	<!-- directive: my-menu Products -->

If you wanted to use your directive as either an element or an attribute, you'd pass *EA* as the `restrict` string.

If you omit the `restrict` property, the default is *A*, and your directive can be used only as an attribute.

If you plan to support IE8, attribute- and class-based directives are your best bet, as it requires extra effort to make new elements work properly. See the Angular documentation (*http://docs.angularjs.org/guide/directive*) for full details on this.

Priorities

In cases where you have multiple directives on a single DOM element and where the order in which they're applied matters, you can use the `priority` property to order their application. Higher numbers run first. The default priority is 0 if you don't specify one.

Needing to set priority will likely be a rare occurrence. One example of a directive that needs to set priority is the `ng-repeat`. When repeating elements, we want Angular to make copies of the template element before other directives get applied. Without this, the other directives would get applied to the canonical template element rather than to the repeated elements we want in our app.

Though it's not in the documentation, you can search the Angular source (*https://github.com/angular/angular.js*) for the few other directives that use `priority`. For `ng-`

repeat, we use a priority value of 1000, so there's plenty of room for other priorities beneath it.

Templates

When creating components, widgets, controls, and so on, Angular lets you replace or wrap the contents of an element with a template that you provide. For example, if you were to create a set of tabbed views in your UI, you would render something like Figure 6-1.

Figure 6-1. Tabbed views

Instead of having a bunch of <div>, <ul><li>, and <a> elements, you could create the directives <tab-set> and <tab>, which declare the structure of each tab respectively. Your HTML then does a much better job of expressing the intent of your template. The end result could look like:

```
<tab-set>
  <tab title='Home'>
    <p>Welcome home!</p>
  </tab>
  <tab title='Preferences'>
    <!-- preferences UI goes here -->
  </tab>
</tabset>
```

You could also data bind the strings for title and the tab content via a controller on <tab> or <tabset>. And it's not limited to tabs—you can do menus, accordions, pop-ups, dialog boxes, or anything else your app needs in this way.

You specify the replacement DOM elements either through the template or the templateUrl properties. You'd use template to set the template content via a string, and templateUrl to refer to the template to be loaded from a file on the server. As you'll see in the following example, you can pre-cache these templates to reduce the number of GET requests, potentially improve performance.

Let's write a dumb directive: a <hello> element that just replaces itself with <div>Hi there</div>. In it, we'll set restrict to allow elements and set template to what we want to display. As the default behavior is to append content to elements, we'll set `replace` to true to replace the original template:

```
var appModule = angular.module('app', []);
appModule.directive('hello', function() {
  return {
    restrict: 'E',
    template: '<div>Hi there</div>',
    replace: true
  };
});
```

We'll use it in a page like so:

```
<html lang='en' ng-app='app'>
...
<body>
  <hello></hello>
</body>
...
```

Loading it into a browser, we see "Hi there."

If you were to view the page source, you'd still see the <hello></hello> on the page, but if you inspected the generated source (in Chrome, right-click on *Hi there* and select *Inspect Element*), you would see:

```
<body>
  <div>Hi there</div>
</body>
```

The <hello></hello> was replaced by the <div> from the template.

If you were to remove the `replace: true` from the directive definition, you'd see <hello> Hi there </hello>.

You'll usually want to use `templateUrl` instead of `template`, as typing HTML into strings isn't much fun. The `template` property is usually only useful for very small templates. Writing as `templateUrl` is useful, as these templates are cacheable by setting the appropriate headers. We could rewrite our `hello` directive example like so:

```
var appModule = angular.module('app', []);
appModule.directive('hello', function() {
  return {
    restrict: 'E',
    templateUrl: 'helloTemplate.html',
    replace: true
  };
});
```

and in `helloTemplate.html`, you would put:

```
<div>Hi there</div>
```

If you are using Chrome as your browser, the "same origin policy" will prevent Chrome from loading these templates from *file://*, and you'll get an error that says something like "Origin null is not allowed by Access-Control-Allow-Origin." You have two options here:

- Load your app through a web server
- Set a flag on Chrome. You can do this by running Chrome from the command line as `chrome --allow-file-access-from-files`

Loading these files through `templateUrl` will, however, make your user wait until they load to see the directive. If you want to have the template load with the first page, you can include it as part of the page in a `script` tag, like so:

```
<script type='text/ng-template' id='helloTemplateInline.html'>
  <div>Hi there</div>
</script>
```

The `id` attribute here is important, as this is the URL key that Angular uses to store the template. You'll use this `id` later in your directive's `templateUrl` to specify which template to insert.

This version will load just fine without a server, as no `XMLHttpRequest` is necessary to fetch the content.

Finally, you could load the templates yourself over `$http` or another mechanism and then set them directly in the object Angular uses called the `$templateCache`. We want this template available in the cache before the directives run, so we'll call it via a `run` function on our module.

```
var appModule = angular.module('app', []);

appModule.run(function($templateCache) {
  $templateCache.put('helloTemplateCached.html', '<div>Hi there</div>');
});

appModule.directive('hello', function() {
  return {
    restrict: 'E',
    templateUrl: 'helloTemplateCached.html',
    replace: true
  };
});
```

You would likely want to do this in production only as a technique to reduce the number of GET requests required. You'd run a script to concatenate all the templates into a single file, and load it in a new module that you then reference from your main application module.

Transclusion

In addition to replacing or appending the content, you can also move the original content within the new template through the transclude property. When set to true, the directive will delete the original content, but make it available for reinsertion within your template through a directive called ng-transclude.

We could change our example to use transclusion:

```
appModule.directive('hello', function() {
  return {
    template: '<div>Hi there <span ng-transclude></span></div>',
    transclude: true
  };
});
```

applying it as:

```
<div hello>Bob</div>
```

We would see: "Hi there Bob."

Compile and Link Functions

While inserting templates is useful, the really interesting work of any directive happens in its compile or its link function.

The compile and link functions are named after the two phases Angular uses to create the live view for your application. Let's take a high-level view of Angular's initialization process, in order:

Script loads
> Angular loads and looks for the ng-app directive to find the application boundaries.

Compile phase
> In this phase, Angular walks the DOM to identify all the registered directives in the template. For each directive, it then transforms the DOM based on the directive's rules (template, replace, transclude, and so on), and calls the compile function if it exists. The result is a compiled template function, which will invoke the link functions collected from all of the directives.

Link phase
> To make the view dynamic, Angular then runs a link function for each directive. The link functions typically creates listeners on the DOM or the model. These listeners keep the view and the model in sync at all times.

So we've got the compile phase, which deals with transforming the template, and the link phase, which deals with modifying the data in the view. Along these lines, the primary difference between the compile and link functions in directives is that compile functions deal with transforming the template itself, and `link` functions deal with making a dynamic connection between model and view. It is in this second phase that scopes are attached to the compiled `link` functions, and the directive becomes *live* through data binding.

These two phases are separate for performance reasons. `Compile` functions execute only once in the compile phase, whereas `link` functions are executed many times, once for each instance of the directive. For example, let's say you use `ng-repeat` over your directive. You don't want to call `compile`, which causes a DOM-walk on each `ng-repeat` iteration. Instead, you want to compile once, then `link`.

While you should certainly learn the differences between `compile` and `link` and the capabilities of each, the majority of directives you'll need to write will not need to transform the template; you'll write mostly `link` functions.

Let's take a look at the syntax for each of these again to compare. For `compile`, we have:

```
compile: function compile(tElement, tAttrs, transclude) {
  return {
    pre: function preLink(scope, iElement, iAttrs, controller) { ... },
    post: function postLink(scope, iElement, iAttrs, controller) { ... }
  }
}
```

And for `link`, it is:

```
link: function postLink(scope, iElement, iAttrs) { ... }
```

Notice that one difference here is that the `link` function gets access to a scope but `compile` does not. This is because during the compile phase, the scope doesn't exist yet. You do, however, have the ability to return `link` functions from the `compile` function. These `link` functions do have access to the scope.

Notice also that both `compile` and `link` receive a reference to their DOM element and the list of attributes for that element. The difference here is that the `compile` function receives the `template` element and attributes from the template, and thus gets the *t* prefix. The `link` function receives them from the view instances created from the template, and thus gets the *i* prefix.

This distinction only matters when the directive is within some other directive that makes copies of the template. The `ng-repeat` directive is a good example.

```
<div ng-repeat='thing in things'>
  <my-widget config='thing'></my-widget>
</div>
```

Here, the `compile` function will be called exactly once, but the `link` function will be called once per copy of `my-widget`—equal to the number of elements in `things`. So, if `my-widget` needs to modify something in common to all copies (instances) of `my-widget`, the right place to do this, for efficiency's sake, is in a `compile` function.

You will also notice that the `compile` function receives a `transclude` function as a property. Here, you have an opportunity to write a function that programmatically transcludes content for situations where the simple template-based transclusion won't suffice.

Lastly, `compile` can return both a `preLink` and a `postLink` function, whereas `link` specifies only a `postLink` function. `preLink`, as its name implies, runs after the compile phase, but before directives on the child elements are linked. Similarly, `postLink` runs after all the child element directives are linked. This means that if you need to change the DOM structure, you will do so in `postLink`. Doing it in the `preLink` will confuse the attachment process and cause an error.

Scopes

You will often want to access a scope from your directive to watch model values and make UI updates when they change, and to notify Angular when external events cause the model to change. This is most common when you're wrapping some non-Angular component from jQuery, Closure, or another library, or implementing simple DOM events. Evaluate Angular expressions passed into your directive as attributes.

When you want a scope for one of these reasons, you have three options for the type of scope you'll get:

1. The **existing scope** from your directive's DOM element.
2. A **new scope** you create that inherits from your enclosing controller's scope. Here, you'll have the ability to read all the values in the scopes above this one in the tree. This scope will be shared with any other directives on your DOM element that request this kind of scope and can be used to communicate with them.
3. An **isolate scope** that inherits no model properties from its parent. You'll want to use this option when you need to isolate the operation of this directive from the parent scope when creating reusable components.

You can create these scope configurations with the following syntax:

Scope Type	Syntax
existing scope	`scope: false` (this is the default if unspecified)
new scope	`scope: true`
isolate scope	`scope: { /* attribute names and binding style */ }`

When you create an isolate scope, you don't have access to anything in the parent scope's model by default. You can, however, specify that you want specific attributes passed into your directive. You can think of these attribute names as parameters to the function.

Note that while isolate scopes don't inherit model properties, they are still children of their parent scope. Like all other scopes, they have a $parent property that references their parent.

You can pass specific attributes from the parent scope to the isolate scope by passing a map of directive attribute names. There are three possible ways to pass data to and from the parent scope. We call these different ways of passing data "binding strategies." You can also, optionally, specify a local alias for the attribute name.

The syntax without aliases is in the following form:

```
scope: { attributeName1: 'BINDING_STRATEGY',
         attributeName2: 'BINDING_STRATEGY', …
       }
```

With aliases, the form is:

```
scope: { attributeAlias: 'BINDING_STRATEGY' + 'templateAttributeName',
         …
       }
```

The binding strategies are defined by symbols in Table 6-4:

Table 6-4. Binding strategies

Symbol	Meaning
@	Pass this attribute as a string. You can also data bind values from enclosing scopes by using interpolation {{}} in the attribute value.
=	Data bind this property with a property in your directive's parent scope.
&	Pass in a function from the parent scope to be called later.

These are fairly abstract concepts, so let's look at some variations on a concrete example to illustrate. Let's say that we want to create an *expander* directive that shows a title bar that expands to display extra content when clicked.

It would look like Figure 6-2 when closed.

Figure 6-2. Expander in closed state

It would look like Figure 6-3 when opened.

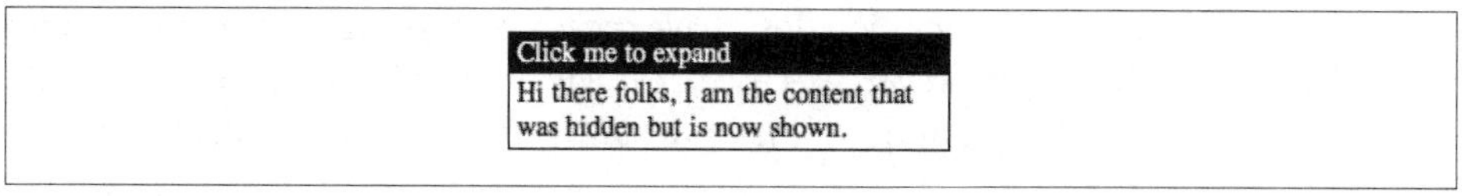

Figure 6-3. Expander in open state

We would write it as follows:

```
<div ng-controller='SomeController'>
  <expander class='expander' expander-title='title'>
    {{text}}
  </expander>
</div>
```

The values for title (*Click me to expand*) and text (*Hi there folks...*), come from the enclosing scope. We could set this up with a controller like so:

```
function SomeController($scope) {
    $scope.title = 'Click me to expand';
    $scope.text = 'Hi there folks, I am the content
                             + 'that was hidden but is now shown.';
}
```

We can then write this directive as:

```
angular.module('expanderModule', [])
  .directive('expander', function(){
    return {
      restrict: 'EA',
      replace: true,
      transclude: true,
      scope: { title:'=expanderTitle' },
      template: '<div>' +
          '<div class="title" ng-click="toggle()">{{title}}</div>' +
          '<div class="body" ng-show="showMe" ng-transclude></div>' +
          '</div>',
      link: function(scope, element, attrs) {
        scope.showMe = false;

        scope.toggle = function toggle() {
          scope.showMe = !scope.showMe;
        }
      }
    }
  });
```

And for styling, we'd do something like this:

```
.expander {
  border: 1px solid black;
  width: 250px;
}
```

```
.expander > .title {
  background-color: black;
  color: white;
  padding: .1em .3em;
  cursor: pointer;
}
.expander > .body {
  padding: .1em .3em;
}
```

Let's look at what each option in the directive is doing for us, in Table 6-5.

Table 6-5. Functions of elements

Function Name	Description
restrict: EA	Invoke this directive as either an element or attribute. That is, `<expander...>...</expander>` and `<div expander...>...</div>` are equivalent.
replace: true	Replace the original element with the template we provide.
transclude: true	Move the original element's content to another location in the provided template.
scope: { title: =*expanderTitle* }	Create a local scope property called `title` that is data bound to a `parent-scope` property declared in the `expander-title` attribute. Here, we're renaming `expanderTitle` as `title` for convenience. We could have written `scope: { expanderTitle: '=' }` and referred to it as `expanderTitle` within our template instead. But in case other directives also have a `title` attribute, it makes sense to disambiguate our title in the API and just rename it for local use. Also notice here that the naming uses the same camel-case expansion as the directive names themselves do.
template: <'div'> + ...	Declare the template to be inserted for this directive. Note that we're using `ng-click` and `ng-show` to show/hide ourselves and `ng-transclude` to declare where the original content will go. Also note that transcluded content gets access to the parent scope, not the scope of the directive enclosing it.
link: ...	Set up the `showMe` model to track the expander's open/closed state and define the `toggle()` function to be called when users click on the `title` div.

If we think it would make more sense to define the expander title in the template rather than in the model, we can use the string-style attribute passing denoted by an @ symbol in the scope declaration, like this:

```
scope: { title:'@expanderTitle' },
```

In the template we can achieve the same effect with:

```
<expander class='expander' expander-title='Click me to expand'>
  {{text}}
</expander>
```

Note that with this @ strategy we could still data bind the title to our controller's scope by using interpolation :

```
<expander class='expander' expander-title='{{title}}'>
  {{text}}
</expander>
```

Manipulating DOM Elements

The `iElement` or `tElement` passed to the directive's `link` and `compile` functions are wrapped references to the native DOM element. If you have loaded the jQuery library, these are jQuery elements you're already used to working with.

If you're not using jQuery, the elements are inside an Angular-native wrapper called jqLite. This API has a subset of jQuery that we need to create everything in Angular. For many applications, you can do everything you need with this API alone.

If you need direct access to the raw DOM element you can get it by accessing the first element of the object with `element[0]`.

You can see the full list of supported APIs in the Angular docs for `angular.element()` —the function you'd use to create jqLite-wrapped DOM elements yourself. It includes functions like `addClass()`, `bind()`, `find()`, `toggleClass()`, and so on. Again, these are all the most useful core functions from jQuery, but with a much smaller code footprint.

In addition to the jQuery APIs, elements also have Angular-specific functions. These exist whether or not you're using the full jQuery library.

Table 6-6. Angular specific functions on an element

Function	Description
`controller(name)`	When you need to communicate directly with a controller, this function returns the controller attached to the element. If none exists for this element, it walks up the DOM and finds the nearest parent controller instead. The name parameter is optional and is used to specify the name of another directive on this same element. If provided, it will return the controller from that directive. The name should be in the camel-case format as with all directives. That is, `ngModel` instead of `ng-model`.
`injector()`	Gets the injector for the current element or its parent. This allows you to ask for dependencies defined for the modules in these elements.
`scope()`	Returns the scope of the current element or its nearest parent.
`inheritedData()`	As with the jQuery function `data()`, `inheritedData()` sets and gets data on an element in a leak-proof way. In addition to getting data from the current element, it will also walk up the DOM to find a value.

As an example, let's re-implement the previous expander example without the help of `ng-show` and `ng-click`. It would look like the following:

```
angular.module('expanderModule', [])
  .directive('expander', function(){
    return {
      restrict: 'EA',
      replace: true,
      transclude: true,
      scope: { title:'=expanderTitle' },
      template: '<div>' +
          '<div class="title">{{title}}</div>' +
          '<div class="body closed" ng-transclude></div>' +
```

```
          '</div>',
      link: function(scope, element, attrs) {
        var titleElement = angular.element(element.children().eq(0));
        var bodyElement = angular.element(element.children().eq(1));

        titleElement.bind('click', toggle);

        function toggle() {
          bodyElement.toggleClass('closed');
        }
      }
    }
  });
```

We've removed the `ng-click` and `ng-show` directives from the template. Instead, to perform the desired action when users click on the expander title, we'll create a jqLite element from the title element and bind the click event to it with a `toggle()` function as its callback. In `toggle()`, we'll call `toggleClass()` on the expander body element to add or remove a class called `closed`, where we'd set the element to `display: none` with a class like this:

```
.closed {
  display: none;
}
```

Controllers

When you have nested directives that need to communicate with each other, the way to do this is through a controller. A `<menu>` may need to know about the `<menu-item>` elements inside it so it can show and hide them appropriately. The same would be true for a `<tab-set>` knowing about its `<tab>` elements, or a `<grid-view>` knowing about its `<grid-element>` elements.

As previously shown, to create an API to communicate between directives, you can declare a controller as part of a directive with the controller property syntax:

```
controller: function controllerConstructor($scope, $element, $attrs, $transclude)
```

This controller function is dependency injected, so the parameters listed here, while potentially useful, are all optional—they can be listed in any order. They're also only a subset of the services available.

Other directives can have this controller passed to them with the `require` property syntax. The full form of `require` looks like:

```
require: '^?directiveName'
```

Explanations of the `require` string can be found in Table 6-7.

Table 6-7. Options for required controllers

Option	Usage
directiveName	This camel-cased name specifies which directive the controller should come from. So if our `<my-menu-item>` directive needs to find a controller on its parent `<my-menu>`, we'd write it as *myMenu*.
^	By default, Angular gets the controller from the named directive on the same element. Adding this optional ^ symbol says to also walk up the DOM tree to find the directive. For the `<my-menu>` example, we'd need to add this symbol; the final string would be `\^myMenu`.
?	If the required controller is not found, Angular will throw an exception to tell you about the problem. Adding a ? symbol to the string says that this controller is optional and that an exception shouldn't be thrown if not found. Though it sounds unlikely, if we wanted to let `<my-menu-item>`s be used without a `<my-menu>` container, we could add this for a final require string of `?\^myMenu`.

As an example, let's rewrite our expander directive to be used in a set called "accordion," which ensures that when you open one expander, the others in the set automatically close. This looks something like Figure 6-4.

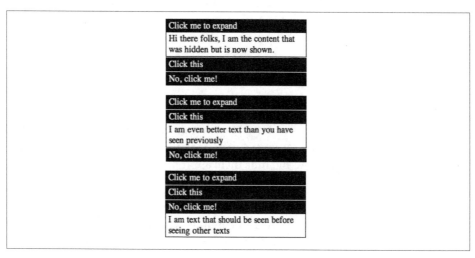

Figure 6-4. Accordion component in multiple states

First, let's write the accordion directive that will do the coordination. We'll add our controller constructor here with methods to do the coordination:

```
appModule.directive('accordion', function() {
  return {
    restrict: 'EA',
    replace: true,
    transclude: true,
    template: '<div ng-transclude></div>',
    controller: function() {
      var expanders = [];
```

```
      this.gotOpened = function(selectedExpander) {
        angular.forEach(expanders, function(expander) {
          if (selectedExpander != expander) {
            expander.showMe = false;
          }
        });
      }

      this.addExpander = function(expander) {
        expanders.push(expander);
      }
    }
  }
});
```

We've defined an addExpander() function for expanders to call to register themselves. We've also created a gotOpened() function for the expanders to call so the accordion's controller can know to close any other open expanders.

In the expander directive itself, we'll extend it to require the accordion's controller from the parent element and call addExpander() and gotOpened() at appropriate times.

```
appModule.directive('expander', function(){
  return {
    restrict: 'EA',
    replace: true,
    transclude: true,
    require: '^?accordion',
    scope: { title:'=expanderTitle' },
    template: '<div>' +
        '<div class="title" ng-click="toggle()">{{title}}</div>' +
        '<div class="body" ng-show="showMe" ng-transclude></div>' +
        '</div>',
    link: function(scope, element, attrs, accordionController) {
      scope.showMe = false;
      accordionController.addExpander(scope);

      scope.toggle = function toggle() {
        scope.showMe = !scope.showMe;
        accordionController.gotOpened(scope);
      }
    }
  }
});
```

Notice that the controller in the accordion directive creates an API through which the expanders can all communicate.

We can then write a template to use these, which will produce the end result in Figure 6-4.

```
<body ng-controller='SomeController' >
  <accordion>
    <expander class='expander'
```

```
      ng-repeat='expander in expanders'
      expander-title='expander.title'>
        {{expander.text}}
      </expander>
    </accordion>
  </body>
```

with an appropriate controller, of course:

```
function SomeController($scope) {
  $scope.expanders = [
    {title: 'Click me to expand',
     text: 'Hi there folks, I am the content that was hidden but is now shown.'},
    {title: 'Click this',
     text: 'I am even better text than you have seen previously'},
    {title: 'No, click me!',
     text: 'I am text that should be seen before seeing other texts'}
  ];
}
```

Moving On

As we've seen, directives let us extend HTML's syntax and turn many application tasks into a do-what-I-mean declaration. Directives make reuse a breeze—from configuring your app, like with `ng-model` and `ng-controller`, to doing template tasks like `ng-repeat` and `ng-view`, to sky's-the-limit reusable components such as data-grids, bubble-charts, tool-tips, and tabs.

CHAPTER 7

Other Concerns

In this chapter, we will take a look at some other useful features that are present in AngularJS, but weren't covered at all or in depth in the chapters and examples so far.

$location

Up to now, you have seen quite a few examples of the $location service in AngularJS. Most of them would have been fleeting glances—an access here, set there. In this section, we will dive into what exactly the $location service in AngularJS is for, and when you should and shouldn't use it.

The $location service is a wrapper around the window.location that is present in any browser. So why would you want to use it instead of working directly with window.location?

Goodbye global state

   window.location is a prime example of global state (actually, both window and document objects in the browser are prime examples). The minute you have global state in your application, testing, maintaining and working with it becomes a hassle (if not now, then definitely in the long run). The $location service hides this nastiness (what we call global state), and allows you to test the browser's location details by injecting mocks during your unit tests.

API

   window.location gives you total access to the contents of the browser location. That is, window.location gives you the string while $location gives you nice, jQuery-like setters and getters to work with it in a clean way.

AngularJS integration

If you use $location, you can use it however you want. But with window.loca
tion, you would have to be responsible for notifying AngularJS of changes, and
listen to changes as well.

HTML5 integration

The $location service is smart enough to realize when HTML5 APIs are available
within a browser and use them. If they're not available, it will fall back to the default
usage.

So when should you use the $location service? Any time you want to react to a change
in the URL (that is not covered by the $routes, which you should primarily use for
working with URL-based views), as well as effect a change in the current URL in the
browser.

Let's consider a small example of how you would use the $location service in a real-
world application. Consider a case where we have a datepicker, and when a date is
selected, the app navigates to a certain URL. Let us take a look at how that might look:

```
// Assume that the datepicker calls $scope.dateSelected with the date
$scope.dateSelected = function(dateTxt) {
    $location.path('/filteredResults?startDate=' + dateTxt);
    // If this were being done in the callback for
    // an external library, like jQuery, then we would have to
    $scope.$apply();
};
```

To $apply, or Not to $apply?

There is confusion amongst AngularJS developers about when $scope.$apply() should
be called and when it shouldn't. Recommendations and rumors on the Internet are
rampant. This section will make it crystal clear.

But first, let us try to put $apply in a simpler form.

Scope.$apply is like a lazy worker. It is told to do a lot of work, and it is responsible for
making sure that the bindings are updated and the view reflects all those changes. But
rather than doing this work all the time, it does it only when it feels it has enough work
to be done. In all other cases, it just nods, and notes the work for later. It only actually
does the work when you get its attention and tell it explicitly to work. AngularJS does
this internally at regular intervals within its lifecycle, but if the call comes from outside
(say a jQuery UI event), scope.$apply just takes note, but does nothing. That is why
we have to call scope.$apply to tell it, "Hey! You need to do this right now, and not
wait!"

Here are four quick tips about when (and how) to call $apply.

- **DO NOT** call it all the time. Calling `$apply` when AngularJS is happily ticking away (in its `$digest` cycle, as we call it) will cause an exception. So "better safe than sorry" is not the approach you want to use.

- **DO CALL** it when controls outside of AngularJS (DOM events, external callbacks such as jQuery UI controls, and so on) are calling AngularJS functions. At that point, you want to tell AngularJS to update itself (the models, the views, and so on), and `$apply` does just that.

- Whenever possible, execute your code or function by passing it to `$apply`, rather than executing the function and then calling `$apply()`. For example, execute the following code:

```
$scope.$apply(function() {
  $scope.variable1 = 'some value';
  executeSomeAction();
});
```

instead of the following:

```
$scope.variable1 = 'some value';
executeSomeAction();
$scope.$apply();
```

While both of these will have the same effect, they differ in one significant way.

The first will capture any errors that happen when `executeSomeAction` is called, while the latter will quietly ignore any such errors. You will get error notifications from AngularJS only when you do the first.

- Consider using something like safeApply (*https://coderwall.com/p/ngisma*):

```
$scope.safeApply = function(fn) {
  var phase = this.$root.$$phase;
  if(phase == '$apply' || phase == '$digest') {
    if(fn && (typeof(fn) === 'function')) {
      fn();
    }
  } else {
    this.$apply(fn);
  }
};
```

You can monkey patch this into the topmost scope or the rootscope, and then use the `$scope.$safeApply` function everywhere. This has been under discussion, and hopefully in a future release, this will be the default behavior.

What are those other methods also available on the `$location` object? Table 7-1 contains a quick summary for you to use in a bind.

Let us take a look at how the $location service would behave, if the URL in the browser was *http://www.host.com/base/index.html#!/path?param1=value1#hashValue*.

Table 7-1. Functions on the $location service

Getter Function	Getter Value	Setter Function
absUrl()	*http://www.host.com/base/index.html#!/path?param1=value1#hashValue*	N/A
hash()	hashValue	hash('newHash')
host()	*www.host.com*	N/A
path()	/path	path('/newPath')
protocol()	http	N/A
search()	{'a': 'b'}	search({'c': 'def'})
url()	/path?param1=value1?hashValue	url('/newPath?p2=v2')

The Setter Function column in Table 7-1 has some sample values that denote the type of object the setter function expects.

Note that the search() setter has a few modes of operation:

- Calling search(searchObj) with an object<string, string> basically denotes all the parameters and their values
- Calling search(string) will set the URL params as q=String directly in the URL
- Calling search(param, value) with a string and value sets (or calling with null removes) a particular search parameter in the URL

Using any one of the setters does not mean that window.location will get changed instantly! The $location service plays well with the Angular lifecycle, so all changes to the location will accumulate and get applied together at the end of the cycle. So feel free to make those changes, one after the other, without fear that the user will see a URL that keeps flickering and changing underneath him.

HTML5 Mode and Hashbang Mode

The $location service can be configured using the $locationProvider (which can be injected, just like everything else in AngularJS). Of particular interest are two properties on this provider, which are:

html5Mode
> A boolean value which dictates whether the $location service works in HTML5 mode or not

hashPrefix
> A string value (actually a single character) that is used as the prefix for Hashbang URLs (in Hashbang mode or legacy browsers in HTML5 mode). By default it is

empty, so Angular's hash is just ''. If the `hashPrefix` is set to '!', then Angular uses what we call Hashbang URLs (! followed by the url).

You might ask, just what are these modes? Well, pretend that you have this super awesome website at *www.superawesomewebsite.com* that uses AngularJS.

Let's say you have a particular route (with some parameters and a hash), such as */foo?bar=123#baz*.

In normal Hashbang mode (with the `hashPrefix` set to '!'), or in legacy browsers without HTML5 mode support, your URL would look something like:

```
http://www.superawesomewebsite.com/#!/foo?bar=123#baz
```

While in HTML5 mode, the URL would simply look like this:

```
http://www.superawesomewebsite.com/foo?bar=123#baz
```

In both cases, `location.path()` would be /foo, `location.search()` would be bar=123, and `location.hash()` would be baz. So if that is the case, why wouldn't you want to use the HTML5 mode?

The Hashbang approach works seamlessly across all browsers, and requires the least amount of configuration. You just need to set the `hashBang` prefix (! by default) and you are good to go.

The HTML5 mode, on the other hand, talks to the browser URL through the use of HTML5 History API. The `$location` service is smart enough to figure out whether HTML5 mode is supported or not, and fall back to the Hashbang approach if necessary, so you don't need to worry about additional work. But you do have to take care of the following:

Server-side configuration

Because HTML5 links look like any other URL on your application, you need to take care on the server side to route all links within your app to your main HTML (most likely, the *index.html*). For example, if your app is the landing page for *superawesomewebsite.com*, and you have a route `/amazing?who=me` in your app, then the URL that the browser would show is *http://www.superawesomewebsite.com/amazing?who=me+*.

When you browse through your app, this will be fine, as the HTML5 History API kicks in and takes care of things. But if you try to browse directly to this URL, your server will look at you as if you have gone crazy, as there is no such known resource on its side. So you would have to ensure that all requests to */amazing* get redirected to */index.html#!/amazing*.

AngularJS will kick in from that point onward and take care of things. It will detect changes to the path and redirect to the correct AngularJS routes that were defined.

Link rewriting

You can easily specify URLs as follows:

```
<a href="/some?foo=bar">link</a>
```

Depending on whether you are using HTML5 mode or not, AngularJS will take care to redirect to *some?foo=bar* or *index.html#!/some?foo=bar*, respectively. No additional steps are required on your part. Awesome, isn't it?

But the following types of links will not be rewritten, and the browser will perform a full reload on the page:

a. Links that contain a `target element` such as the following:

```
<a href="/some/link" target="_self">link</a>
```

b. Absolute links going to a different domain:

```
<a href="http://www.angularjs.org">link</a>
```

This is different because it is an absolute URL, while the previous example used the existing base URL.

c. Links starting with a different base path when one is already defined:

```
<a href="/some-other-base/link">link</a>
```

Relative Links

Be sure to check all relative links, images, scripts, and so on. You must either specify the URL base in the head of your main HTML file (`<base href="/my-base">`), or you must use absolute URLs (starting with /) everywhere because relative URLs will be resolved to absolute URLs using the initial absolute URL of the document, which is often different from the root of the application.

Running Angular apps with the History API enabled from document root is strongly encouraged, as it takes care of all relative link issues.

AngularJS Module Methods

The AngularJS Module is responsible for defining how your application is bootstrapped. It also declaratively defines the pieces of your application. Let us take a look at how it accomplishes this.

Where's the Main Method?

Those of you coming from a programming language like Java or even Python might be wondering, where is that main method in AngularJS? You know, the one that bootstraps everything, and is the first thing to get executed? The one that functions in JavaScript and instantiates and wires everything together, then tells your application to go run?

AngularJS doesn't have that. What it has instead is the concept of modules. Modules allow us to declaratively specify our application's dependencies, and how the wiring and bootstrapping happens. The reason for this kind of approach is manifold:

1. It is **declarative**. That means it is written in a way that is easier to write and understand. It reads like English!

2. It is **modular**. It forces you to think about how you define your components and dependencies, and makes them explicit.

3. It allows for **easy testing**. In your unit tests, you can selectively pull in modules, and avoid the untestable portions of your code. And in your scenario tests, you can load additional modules, which can make working with some components easier.

Let us first take a look at how you would use a module that you have defined, then take a look at how we would declare one.

Say we have a module, in fact, the module for our application, called "MyAwesomeApp." In my HTML, I could just add the following to the <html> tag (or technically, any other tag):

```
<html ng-app="MyAwesomeApp">
```

The ng-app directive tells AngularJS to bootstrap your application using the MyAwesomeApp module.

So how would that module be defined? Well, for one, we recommend that you have separate modules for your services, directives, and filters. Your main module could then just declare the other modules as a dependency (just like we did in Chapter 4 with the RequireJS example).

This makes it easier to manage your modules, as they are nice complete chunks of code. Each module has one and only one responsibility. This also allows your tests to load only the modules they care about, and thus reduces the amount of initialization that needs to happen. The tests can be small and focused.

Loading and Dependencies

Module loading happens in two distinct phases, and the functions reflect them. These are the Config and the Run blocks (or phases):

The Config block

AngularJS hooks up and registers all the providers in this phase. Because of this, only providers and constants can be injected into Config blocks. Services that may or may not have been initialized cannot be injected.

The Run block

Run blocks are used to kickstart your application, and start executing after the injector is finished creating. To prevent further system configuration from happening from this point onwards, only instances and constants can be injected into Run blocks. The Run block is the closest you are going to find to a main method in AngularJS.

Convenience Methods

What can you do with a module? We can instantiate controllers, directives, filters, and services, but the module class allows you to do more, as you can see in Table 7-2:

Table 7-2. Module configuration methods

API Method	Description
config(configFn)	Use this method to register work that needs to be done when the module is loading.
constant(name, object)	This happens first, so you can declare all your constants app-wide, and have them available at all configuration (the first method in this list) and instance methods (all methods from here on, like controller, service, and so on).
controller(name, constructor)	We have seen a lot of examples of this; it basically sets up a controller for use.
directive(name, directiveFactory)	As discussed in Chapter 6, this allows you to create directives within your app.
filter(name, filterFactory)	Allows you to create named AngularJS filters, as discussed in previous chapters.
run(initializationFn)	Use this method when you want to perform work that needs to happen once the injector is set up, right before your application is available to the user.
value(name, object)	Allows values to be injected across the application.
service(name, serviceFactory)	Covered in the next section.
factory(name, factoryFn)	Covered in the next section.
provider(name, providerFn)	Covered in the next section.

You might realize that we are missing the details of three particular API calls—Factory, Provider, and Service—from the preceding table. There is a reason for that: it is quite easy to confuse the usage between the three, so we will dive into a small example that should better illustrate when (and how!) to use each one.

The Factory

The Factory API call is used whenever we have a class or object that needs some amount of logic or parameters before it can be initialized. A Factory is a function that is responsible for creating a certain value (or object). Let us take the example of a greeter function that needs to be initialized with its salutation:

```
function Greeter(salutation) {
  this.greet = function(name) {
```

```
    return salutation + ' ' + name;
  };
}
```

The greeter factory would look something like:

```
myApp.factory('greeter', function(salut) {
  return new Greeter(salut);
});
```

and it would be called as:

```
var myGreeter = greeter('Halo');
```

The Service

What about services? Well, the difference between a Factory and a Service is that the Factory invokes the function passed to it and returns a result. The Service invokes "new" on the constructor method passed to it and returns the result.

So the preceding greeter Factory could be replaced with a greeter Service as follows:

```
myApp.service('greeter', Greeter);
```

Every time I asked for a greeter, AngularJS would call the new Greeter() and return that.

The Provider

This is the most complicated (and thus most configurable, obviously) of the lot. The Provider combines both the Factory and the Service, and also throws in the benefit of being able to configure the Provider function before the injection system is fully in place (in the config blocks, that is).

Let's see how a modified greeter Service using the Provider might look:

```
myApp.provider('greeter', function() {
  var salutation = 'Hello';
  this.setSalutation = function(s) {
    salutation = s;
  }

  function Greeter(a) {
    this.greet = function() {
      return salutation + ' ' + a;
    }
  }

  this.$get = function(a) {
    return new Greeter(a);
  };
});
```

This allows us to set the salutation at runtime (for example, based on the language of the user).

```
var myApp = angular.module(myApp, []).config(function(greeterProvider) {
  greeterProvider.setSalutation('Namaste');
});
```

AngularJS would internally call $get whenever someone asked for an instance of the greeter object.

 Warning!
There is a slight, but significant difference between using:

```
angular.module('MyApp', [...])
```

and:

```
angular.module('MyApp')
```

The difference is that the first creates a new Angular module, pulling in the module dependencies listed in the square brackets ([...]). The second uses the existing module that has already been defined by the first call.

So you should make sure that you use the following code only once in your entire application:

```
angular.module('MyApp', [...])   // Or MyModule, if you are modularizing your app
```

If you do not plan to save it to a variable and refer to it across your application, then use angular.module(MyApp) in the rest of the files to ensure you get a handle to the correct AngularJS module. Everything on the module must be defined by accessing the variable, or be added on the spot where the module has been defined.

Communicating Between Scopes with $on, $emit, and $broadcast

AngularJS scopes have a very hierarchical and nested structure. There is one main $rootScope (per Angular app or ng-app, that is), which all other scopes either inherit, or are nested under. Quite often, you will find that scopes don't share variables or do not prototypically inherit from one another.

In such a case, how do you communicate between scopes? One option is creating a service that is a singleton in the scope of the app, and processing all inter-scope communication through that service.

There is another option in AngularJS: communicating through events on the scope. There are some restrictions; for example, you cannot generally broadcast an event to all watching scopes. You have to be selective in whether you are communicating to your parents or to your children.

But before we discuss that, how do you listen to these events? Here is an example where our scope on any Star System is waiting and watching for an event we call "planetDestroyed."

```
scope.$on('planetDestroyed', function(event, galaxy, planet) {
  // Custom event, so what planet was destroyed
  scope.alertNearbyPlanets(galaxy, planet);
});
```

Where do these additional arguments to the event listener come from? Let's take a look at how an individual planet could communicate with its parent Star System.

```
scope.$emit('planetDestroyed', scope.myGalaxy, scope.myPlanet);
```

The additional arguments to $emit are passed on as function parameters to the listener functions. Also, $emit communicates only upwards from its current scope, so the poor denizens of the planet (if they had a scope to themselves) would not be notified if their planet was being destroyed.

Similarly, if a Galaxy wanted to communicate downwards to its child, the Star System scope, then it could communicate as follows:

```
scope.$emit('selfDestructSystem', targetSystem);
```

Then all Star Systems listening for the event could look at the target system, and decide if they should self-destruct, using these commands:

```
scope.$on('selfDestructSystem', function(event, targetSystem) {
    if (scope.mySystem === targetSystem) {
        scope.selfDestruct();   // Go Ka-boom!!
    }
});
```

Of course, as the event propagates all the way up (or down), it might become necessary at a certain level or scope to say, "Enough! You shall not PASS!" or to prevent what the event does by default. The event object passed to the listener has functions to handle all of the above, and more, so let us take a quick look at what you can get up to with the event object in Table 7-3.

Table 7-3. Event object properties and methods

Property of event	Purpose
event.targetScope	The scope which emitted or broadcasted the event originally
event.currentScope	The scope currently handling the event
event.name	The name of the event
event.stopPropagation()	A function which will prevent further event propagation (this is available only for events that were $emitted
event.preventDefault()	This actually doesn't do anything but set defaultPrevented to true. It is up to the implementer of the listeners to check on defaultPrevented before taking action
event.defaultPrevented	true if preventDefault was called

Cookies

Before long, you will encounter a situation in your application (provided it is sufficiently large and complex) where you need to store some kind of state across users' sessions on the client side. You might remember (or have nightmares) about working with plain-text cookies through the *document.cookie* interface.

Thankfully, many years have passed since then, and HTML5 APIs are available in almost all the modern browsers that are currently out there. Moreover, AngularJS provides you with a nice $cookie and $cookieStore API to work with cookies. Both services play nice with HTML5 cookies (*http://www.w3schools.com/html/html5_webstorage.asp*), in that they use HTML5 APIs when available, and default to working with document.cookies when they are not. Either way, you get to use the same API calls.

Let's take a look at the $cookies service first. $cookies is simply an object. It has keys and values. Adding a key and its corresponding value to the object adds the information to the cookie, and removing it from the object deletes that particular cookie. It's as simple as that.

But most of the time, you would not want to work directly at the $cookies level. Working directly at the cookies level would mean doing string manipulation and parsing yourself, and converting data to and from objects. For those cases, we have the $cookieStore, which provides a programmatic way of writing and removing cookies. So what would a Search Controller that remembers the last five search results using the $cookieStore look like?

```
function SearchController($scope, $cookieStore) {
  $scope.search = function(text) {
    // Do the search here
    ...
    // Get the past results, or initialize an empty array if nothing found
    var pastSearches = $cookieStore.get('myapp.past.searches') || [];
    if (pastSearches.length > 5) {
      pastSearches = pastSearches.splice(0);
    }
    pastSearches.push(text);
    $cookieStore.put('myapp.past.searches', pastSearches);
  };
}
```

Internationalization and Localization

You might have heard people throw about both terms when it comes to supporting your application in different languages. But there is a slight difference between the two. Consider a simple application that is a portal into your bank balance. Every time you come into the application, it displays one and only one thing:

```
Greetings! The balance in your account as of 10/25/2012 is $XX,XXX.
```

Now, obviously, the preceding code is targeted at an American audience. But what if we wanted this application to be available in the UK as well (just so that the language itself doesn't change)? Britain uses a different date format and currency symbol, but you don't want your code to undergo a change every time you need the application to support a new locale (in this case, en_US and en_UK). This process of abstracting out the date/time format, as well as the currency symbol, from your coding logic is known as *Internationalization* (or i18n—the 18 denoting the number of letters between i and n in the word).

What if we wanted to support the application in Hindi? Or Russian? In addition to the date format and the currency symbol (and formatting), even the strings used in the UI would have to change. This process of providing translations and localized strings for the abstracted bits in various locales is known as *Localization* (or L10n—with a capital L to differentiate between i and l).

What Can I Do in AngularJS?

AngularJS supports i18n/L10n for the following filters out of the box:

- currency
- date/time
- number

There is also pluralization support (for English as well as i18n/L10n) with the ngPlur alize directive.

All of this pluralization support is handled and managed by the $locale service, which manages the locale-specific rule sets. The $locale service works off of locale IDs, which generally consist of two parts: the country code and the language code. For example, en_US and en_UK, denote English used in the US and the UK, respectively. Specifying a country code is optional, just specifying "en" is a valid locale code.

How Do I Get It All Working?

Getting L10n and i18n working in AngularJS is a three-step process:

Index.html changes
  AngularJS requires you to have a separate *index.html* for each supported locale. Your server also needs to know which *index.html* it has to provide, depending on the user's locale preferences (this could also be triggered from a client-side change, when the user changes his locale).

Creating localized rule sets

> The next step is creating an *angular.js* file for each supported locale, like (*angular_en-US.js* and *angular_zh-CN.js*). This involves concatenating the localization rules for each particular language (the default files for the preceding two locales would be *angular-locale_en-US.js* and *angular-locale_zh-CN.js*) at the end of the *angular.js* or the *angular.min.js* file. So your *angular_en-US.js* would contain the contents of *angular.js* first, followed by the contents of the *angular-locale_en-US.js*.

Sourcing the localized rule sets

> The final step involves ensuring that your localized *index.html* refers to the localized rule set instead of the original *angular.js* file. So *index_en-US.html* should use *angular-en_US.js* and not *angular.js*.

What about my UI strings, you ask? AngularJS currently doesn't have its own full-fledged translation APIs yet, so you will have to come up with your own techniques and scripts to get the UI strings translated. This could be something that parses your HTML for strings, and is then fed to a translator to churn out an HTML for each language, or something much more complex and specific based on your need.

Common Gotchas

Translation Length

> You design your UI so that it shows June 24, 1988 in a div that has been painstakingly sized to fit it just right. And then you open your UI in Spanish. 24 de junio de 1988 just doesn't fit in that same space anymore…

> When internationalizing your apps, keep in mind that the lengths of your strings might change drastically from language to language. Design your CSS accordingly, and do thorough testing across the various languages. (Don't forget that right to left languages also exist!)

Timezones

> The AngularJS date/time filter picks up the timezone settings from the browser. So depending on the timezone of the computer, different people might see different information. Neither JS nor AngularJS have any built-in support to display time with a timezone specified by the developer.

Sanitizing HTML & the Sanitize Module

AngularJS takes its security seriously, and tries to make all efforts to ensure that most attack vectors are minimized. One of the attack vectors revolves around the injection of unsafe HTML content into your webpage and using that to trigger a cross-site or injection attack.

Consider the example where we have a variable on the scope called myUnsafeHTMLContent. OnMouseOver modifies the contents of the element to "PWN3D!" if the HTML is used as is:

```
$scope.myUnsafeHTMLContent = '<p style="color:blue">an html' +
    '<em onmouseover="this.textContent = 'PWN3D!'">click here</em>' +
    'snippet</p>';
```

The default behavior in AngularJS, when you have some HTML content in a variable and try to bind to it, would result in AngularJS escaping your content and printing it as is. So the HTML content ends up getting treated as pure text.

Therefore:

```
<div ng-bind='myUnsafeHTMLContent'></div>
```

will result in:

```
<p style="color:blue">an html
<em onmouseover="this.textContent='PWN3D!'">click here</em>
snippet</p>
```

getting rendered as text on your web page.

But what if you wanted to render the contents of myUnsafeHTMLContents as HTML in your AngularJS app? In such a case, AngularJS has additional directives (and a service, $sanitize, to boot) to allow you to render the HTML in both a safe and unsafe manner.

Let us first take the example where you want to be safe (as you normally should be!), and render the HTML, taking care to get rid of most possible attack vectors in the HTML. You would use the ng-bind-html directive in such a case.

The ng-bind-html, ng-bind-html-unsafe, and linky filter all are in the ngSanitize module. You will need to include *angular-sanitize.js* (or *.min.js*) in your script dependencies, and then add a module dependency to ngSanitize, before any of these work.

So what happens when we use the ng-bind-html directive on the same myUnsafeHTMLContent, like so?

```
<div ng-bind-html="myUnsafeHTMLContent"></div>
```

The output in such a case would be the following:

```
an html _click here_ snippet
```

The important things to note are that the style tag (with color blue), and the onmouseover handler on the <em> tag are both removed by AngularJS. They are deemed unsafe, and thus dropped.

Finally, if you decide that you really want the contents of myUnsafeHTMLContent rendered as is, either because you really trust the source of the content, or for some other reason, then you can use the ng-bind-html-unsafe directive:

```
<div ng-bind-html-unsafe="myUnsafeHTMLContent"></div>
```

The output in such a case would be the following:

```
an html _click here_ snippet
```

The color of the text is blue (as per the style attached to the p tag), and the click here does have an onmouseover registered on it. So the minute your mouse strays anywhere near the click here text, the output would change to:

```
an html PWN3D! snippet
```

As you can see, this is quite unsafe in reality, so be absolutely certain that this is what you want when you decide to use the ng-bind-html-unsafe directive. Someone could just as easily read the user's information and send it to his or her servers.

Linky

The linky filter is also present in the ngSanitize module, and basically allows you to add it to HTML content that is being rendered and convert links that are present in the HTML to anchor tags. It is quite simple to use, so let us take a look at an example:

```
$scope.contents = 'Text with links: http://angularjs.org/ & mailto:us@there.org';
```

Now, if you use the following binding:

```
<div ng-bind-html="contents"></div>
```

this would result in the contents of the HTML getting printed as:

```
Text with links: http://angularjs.org/ & mailto:us@there.org
```

Now let's take a look at what happens when we use the linky filter:

```
<div ng-bind-html="contents | linky"></div>
```

The linky filter goes through the text contents and adds <a> tags to all URLs and *mailto* links it finds, thus providing HTML content that the user can interact with:

```
Text with links: http://angularjs.org/ & us@there.org
```

CHAPTER 8

Cheatsheet and Recipes

By now, we have covered pretty much all the different parts of the Angular, including directives, services, controllers, resources, and so much more. But even we know that sometimes just reading about it isn't enough. And sometimes we don't care about how any of that works, we just want to know how to do that one thing with AngularJS?

In this chapter, we take a stab at giving complete coding samples (with little bits of info and pointers to explain what is happening) for some common problems we tackle in most web apps. They are in no particular order, so feel free to jump to whichever ones you care about, or go through them in order. You are the boss!

The examples covered in this chapter include:

1. Wrapping a jQuery Datepicker
2. The Teams List App: Filtering and Controller Communication
3. File Upload in AngularJS
4. Using socket.IO
5. A Simple Pagination Service
6. Working with Servers

Wrapping a jQuery Datepicker

This example can be found in *chapter8/datepicker* on our GitHub page.

Even before we jump into the code, we have to decide how our component is going to look and work. Let's say we want to define our datepicker in HTML as follows:

```
<input datepicker ng-model="currentDate" select="updateMyText(date)"></input>
```

That is, we want to modify the Input field by adding an attribute datepicker, and adding some more functionality to it (like data binding with the model and the ability to be notified when a date is selected). So how would we go about it?

We will re-use existing functionality, the jQuery UI's datepicker, instead of building a datepicker from scratch. We just need to hook it up to AngularJS and latch onto the hooks it provides:

```
angular.module('myApp.directives', [])
  .directive('datepicker', function() {
    return {
      // Enforce the angularJS default of restricting the directive to
      // attributes only
      restrict: 'A',
      // Always use along with an ng-model
      require: '?ngModel',
      scope: {
        // This method needs to be defined and
        // passed in to the directive from the view controller
        select: '&'        // Bind the select function we refer to the
                           // right scope
      },
      link: function(scope, element, attrs, ngModel) {
        if (!ngModel) return;

        var optionsObj = {};

        optionsObj.dateFormat = 'mm/dd/yy';
        var updateModel = function(dateTxt) {
          scope.$apply(function () {
            // Call the internal AngularJS helper to
            // update the two-way binding
            ngModel.$setViewValue(dateTxt);
          });
        };

        optionsObj.onSelect = function(dateTxt, picker) {
          updateModel(dateTxt);
          if (scope.select) {
            scope.$apply(function() {
              scope.select({date: dateTxt});
            });
          }
        };

        ngModel.$render = function() {
          // Use the AngularJS internal 'binding-specific' variable
          element.datepicker('setDate', ngModel.$viewValue || '');
        };
        element.datepicker(optionsObj);
      }
```

```
    };
  });
```

Most of the code is pretty straightforward, but let us walk through some of the more important bits:

ng-model

We get an `ng-model` attribute passed into the linking function of the directive. The `ng-model` (which is mandatory for the directive to function because of the `require` attribute inside the directive definition) allows us to define how the attribute and object linked to the `ng-model` behave in the context of the directive. There are two things you need to pay attention to:

`ngModel.$setViewValue(dateTxt)`
> This is called when something external to AngularJS (in this case, the `onSelect` of the jQuery UI datepicker) happens. This lets AngularJS know that it has to update the model. This is usually called when a DOM event happens.

`ngModel.$render`
> This is the other part to the `ng-model`. This tells Angular how to update the view when the model changes. In our case, we just pass on to the jQuery UI that the datepicker value has changed.

Binding select

Instead of using the attribute value and evaluating it as a string against the scope (in which case, nested functions and objects won't be accessible), we use function binding (the "&" scope binding). This creates a new function on the scope called `select`, which takes one argument—an object. Each key in this object must match an argument specified in the HTML where the directive is used. The value for that key will be the value passed to the function as that argument. The added advantage is that this decouples the controller implementation from having to know anything about the DOM or the directive. The `callback` function just performs its behavior given certain arguments, and does not need to know about the binding or the updates.

Calling select

Notice that we pass in an `optionsObj` to the datepicker, with an `onSelect` function. jQuery UI is responsible for calling the `onSelect` function, which will usually happen outside of AngularJS' execution context. Of course, when functions like `onSelect` are called, AngularJS has no clue. It is up to us to let AngularJS know that it needs to act on stuff. How do we do that? By using `scope.$apply`.

Now we could just as easily do the `$setViewValue` and call the `scope.select` outside `scope.$apply`, and then just call `scope.$apply()`. But then any exceptions that happen in either of these two steps are silently dropped. If they happen within a `scope.$apply` function, then they are captured by AngularJS.

The Rest of the Example

To complete the example, let us take a look at our controller code, and then the HTML to get it working:

```
var app = angular.module('myApp', ['myApp.directives']);

app.controller('MainCtrl', function($scope) {
  $scope.myText = 'Not Selected';
  $scope.currentDate = '';
  $scope.updateMyText = function(date) {
    $scope.myText = 'Selected';
  };
});
```

Pretty simple stuff. We declare a controller, set some scope variables, and then create a scope method (`updateMyText`) that we will later use for binding to the on-`select` event of the datepicker. On to the HTML next:

```
<!DOCTYPE html>
<html ng-app="myApp">

  <head lang="en">
    <meta charset="utf-8">
    <title>AngularJS Datepicker</title>
    <script
        src="http://ajax.googleapis.com/ajax/libs/jquery/1.8.3/jquery.min.js">
    </script>
    <script src="http://code.jquery.com/ui/1.9.2/jquery-ui.js">
    </script>
    <script
        src="http://ajax.googleapis.com/ajax/libs/angularjs/1.0.3/
            angular.min.js">
    </script>

    <link rel="stylesheet"
        href="http://code.jquery.com/ui/1.9.2/themes/base/jquery-ui.css">
    <script src="datepicker.js"></script>
    <script src="app.js"></script>
  </head>

  <body ng-controller="MainCtrl">
    <input id="dateField"
        datepicker
        ng-model="$parent.currentDate"
        select="updateMyText(date)">
```

```
    <br/>
       {{myText}} - {{currentDate}}
    </body>
</html>
```

Notice how the `select` attribute is specified. There is no value "date" on the scope. But because of the way we have set up our function binding in the directive, AngularJS now knows that the function will take an argument, whose `name` will be "date." This is what we specified as an object when the `onSelect` of the datepicker is called.

> For the `ng-model`, we specify `$parent.currentDate` instead of `currentDate`. Why? Because our directive creates an isolated scope so that we can have the `select` function bound. This makes it so that the `currentDate` is no longer linked by `ng-model` even if we set it. So we have to explicitly tell AngularJS that the `currentDate` it needs to refer to is not in the isolated scope, but in its parent scope.

With this, when you load it up in your browser, you would see a text box that, when clicked, exposes the jQuery UI datepicker. On `select`, it updates the text on the screen from "Not Selected" to "Selected," and your date. The date in the input field is also updated.

The Teams List App: Filtering and Controller Communication

In this example, we tackle multiple things at the same time, but there are two major takeaways:

1. How do you use filters—especially in a clean, simple way—with repeaters?
2. How do you communicate between controllers that do not share an inheritance relation?

The app itself is quite simple. There is data, which is a list of teams from various sport, such as basketball, football (the NFL kind, not the soccer kind), and hockey. For each of these teams, we have the name, the city, the sport, and whether the team is featured or not.

What we want to do is display this list, and also display filters on the left that immediately update the list as you modify them. We are going to have two controllers: one for storing the data, and the other to work with the filters. And we are going to use a service to communicate the changes to the filter between the `ListCtrl` and the `FilterCtrl`.

Let us take a look at the service first, which is going to drive the application:

```
angular.module('myApp.services', []).
  factory('filterService', function() {
```

```
      return {
        activeFilters: {},
        searchText: ''
      };
    });
```

Whoa. That's it, you ask? Yes. What we are doing here is leveraging the fact that Angu‐
larJS services are singleton (that's singleton with a small "s"—singleton within the scope,
but not globally visible or accessible). When we declare the filterService, we are guar‐
anteed to have only one instance of the filterService for the entire myApp.

We then end up using the filterService as a communication channel between the Fil
terCtrl and the ListCtrl, as both can bind to it and access stuff as it is updated. Both
of these controllers are actually dead simple, as they do nothing but simple assignment:

```
var app = angular.module('myApp', ['myApp.services']);

app.controller('ListCtrl', function($scope, filterService) {
  $scope.filterService = filterService;
  $scope.teamsList = [{
      id: 1, name: 'Dallas Mavericks', sport: 'Basketball',
      city: 'Dallas', featured: true
    }, {
      id: 2, name: 'Dallas Cowboys', sport: 'Football',
      city: 'Dallas', featured: false
    }, {
      id: 3, name: 'New York Knicks', sport: 'Basketball',
      city: 'New York', featured: false
    }, {
      id: 4, name: 'Brooklyn Nets', sport: 'Basketball',
      city: 'New York', featured: false
    }, {
      id: 5, name: 'New York Jets', sport: 'Football',
      city: 'New York', featured: false
    }, {
      id: 6, name: 'New York Giants', sport: 'Football',
      city: 'New York', featured: true
    }, {
      id: 7, name: 'Los Angeles Lakers', sport: 'Basketball',
      city: 'Los Angeles', featured: true
    }, {
      id: 8, name: 'Los Angeles Clippers', sport: 'Basketball',
      city: 'Los Angeles', featured: false
    }, {
      id: 9, name: 'Dallas Stars', sport: 'Hockey',
      city: 'Dallas', featured: false
    }, {
      id: 10, name: 'Boston Bruins', sport: 'Hockey',
      city: 'Boston', featured: true
    }
  ];
});
```

```
app.controller('FilterCtrl', function($scope, filterService) {
  $scope.filterService = filterService;
});
```

You might be wondering, where is the complexity? AngularJS does make it this easy. All we have left to do is to pull this all together in the template:

```
<!DOCTYPE html>
<html ng-app="myApp">

<head lang="en">
  <meta charset="utf-8">
  <title>Teams List App</title>
  <script src="http://ajax.googleapis.com/ajax/libs/jquery/1.8.3/jquery.min.js">
  </script>
  <script
    src="http://ajax.googleapis.com/ajax/libs/angularjs/1.0.3/angular.min.js">
  </script>
  <link rel="stylesheet"
      href="http://cdnjs.cloudflare.com/ajax/libs/twitter-bootstrap/2.1.1/
      css/bootstrap.min.css">
  <script
      src="http://cdnjs.cloudflare.com/ajax/libs/twitter-bootstrap/2.1.1/
      bootstrap.min.js">
  </script>
  <script src="services.js"></script>
  <script src="app.js"></script>
</head>

<body>
<div class="row-fluid">
  <div class="span3" ng-controller="FilterCtrl">
    <form class="form-horizontal">

      <div class="controls-row">
        <label for="searchTextBox" class="control-label">Search:</label>
        <div class="controls">
          <input type="text"
                 id="searchTextBox"
                 ng-model="filterService.searchText">
        </div>
      </div>

      <div class="controls-row">
        <label for="sportComboBox" class="control-label">Sport:</label>
        <div class="controls">
          <select id="sportComboBox"
                  ng-model="filterService.activeFilters.sport">
            <option ng-repeat="sport in ['Basketball', 'Hockey', 'Football']">
              {{sport}}
            </option>
          </select>
```

```
          </div>
        </div>

      <div class="controls-row">
        <label for="cityComboBox" class="control-label">City:</label>
        <div class="controls">
          <select id="cityComboBox"
                  ng-model="filterService.activeFilters.city">
            <option ng-repeat="city in ['Dallas', 'Los Angeles',
                                        'Boston', 'New York']">
              {{city}}
            </option>
          </select>
        </div>
      </div>

      <div class="controls-row">
        <label class="control-label">Featured:</label>
        <div class="controls">
          <input type="checkbox"
                 ng-model="filterService.activeFilters.featured"
                 ng-false-value="" />
        </div>
      </div>
    </form>
  </div>
  <div class="offset1 span8" ng-controller="ListCtrl">
    <table>
      <thead>
      <tr>
        <th>Name</th>
        <th>Sport</th>
        <th>City</th>
        <th>Featured</th>
      </tr>
      </thead>
      <tbody id="teamListTable">
      <tr ng-repeat="team in teamsList | filter:filterService.activeFilters |
                     filter:filterService.searchText">
        <td>{{team.name}}</td>
        <td>{{team.sport}}</td>
        <td>{{team.city}}</td>
        <td>{{team.featured}}</td>
      </tr>
      </tbody>
    </table>
  </div>
</div>
</body>
</html>
```

There are really only four items of interest in this entire HTML template. Everything else you have seen a few dozen times by now (even these items have been there in some form or another). Let us go over them one by one.

The Search Box

The search box just binds to the `filterService.searchText` field using an `ng-model`. In and of itself, it is nothing noteworthy, but the way this is later used in the filter makes this step essential.

The Combo Boxes

There are two combo boxes, even though we have only highlighted the first. Both of them work the same way. They are both bound to `filterService.activeFil ters.sports` or `city` (depending on the box), which basically sets the sports (or city) property on the filters object in the `filtersService`.

The Check Box

The check box binds to `filterService.activeFilters.featured`. The thing to note is that when featured is checked, we want to show only those teams with `featured = true`. When it is unchecked, we want to show teams with `featured = true` and `featured = false`. For this, we use the `ng-false-value=""` directive to say that the `featured` filter should be cleared when the checkbox is unchecked.

The Repeater

Let us take a look at the `ng-repeat` statement one more time:

```
"team in teamsList | filter:filterService.activeFilters |
    filter:filterService.searchText"
```

The first part is the same as always. It is the two new filters that make all the difference. The first filter tells AngularJS to filter the list using `filterService.activeFilters`. This basically takes each property in the object filters and ensures that each item in the repeater matches corresponding properties in the filter. So if `activeFilters[city]` = *Dallas*, then only those items in the repeater with *city* = Dallas will be selected. If there are multiple filters, then all of them would have to match.

The second filter is a textual match filter. It basically selects only those items that have the value of `filterService.searchText` present in any of their values. So it will do a match across cities, team names, sports, and featured.

File Upload in AngularJS

Another common use case we have seen is to support uploading of files from within an AngularJS app. While it is possible to support this by building on the existing input type "file" that is present in HTML, for the purpose of this example, we are going to extend existing solutions for file upload. A great one is BlueImp's File Upload (*https://github.com/blueimp/jQuery-File-Upload*), which uses jQuery and jQueryUI (or Bootstrap). Their API is dead simple, which also makes our directive super easy.

So let us start with the directive declaration:

```
angular.module('myApp.directives', [])
  .directive('fileupload', function() {
  return {
    restrict: 'A',
    scope: {
      done: '&',
      progress: '&'
    },
    link: function(scope, element, attrs) {
      var optionsObj = {
        dataType: 'json'
      };

      if (scope.done) {
        optionsObj.done = function() {
          scope.$apply(function() {
            scope.done({e: e, data: data});
          });
        };
      }

      if (scope.progress) {
        optionsObj.progress = function(e, data) {
          scope.$apply(function() {
            scope.progress({e: e, data: data});
          });
        }
      }

      // the above could easily be done in a loop, to cover
      // all API's that Fileupload provides

      element.fileupload(optionsObj);
    }
  };
});
```

This code allows us to define our directive in a very simple manner, as well as add hooks for onDone and onProgress. We use function binding so that AngularJS always calls the right methods and uses the right scope.

This is done by the isolated scope declaration, which has two bindings: one for progress and one for done. This creates a function which takes a single argument (an object) on the scope. For instance, scope.done takes an object as an argument. This object has two keys, e and data. These are passed along as arguments to the original function, which we will see in the next section.

Let's take a look at our HTML to see how we would use this:

```
<!DOCTYPE html>
<html ng-app="myApp">

  <head lang="en">
    <meta charset="utf-8">
    <title>File Upload with AngularJS</title>
    <!-- Because we are loading jQuery before AngularJS,
         Angular will use the jQuery library instead of
         its own jQueryLite implementation -->
    <script
      src="http://ajax.googleapis.com/ajax/libs/jquery/1.8.3/jquery.min.js">
    </script>
    <script
      src="http://raw.github.com/blueimp/jQuery-File-Upload/master/js/vendor/
           jquery.ui.widget.js">
    </script>
    <script
      src="http://raw.github.com/blueimp/jQuery-File-Upload/master/js/
           jquery.iframe-transport.js">
    </script>
    <script
      src="http://raw.github.com/blueimp/jQuery-File-Upload/master/js/
           jquery.fileupload.js">
    </script>

    <script
      src="//ajax.googleapis.com/ajax/libs/angularjs/1.0.3/angular.min.js">
    </script>
    <script src="app.js"></script>
  </head>

  <body ng-controller="MainCtrl">
    File Upload:
      <!-- We will define uploadFinished in MainCtrl and attach
           it to the scope, so that it is available here -->
      <input id="testUpload"
             type="file"
             fileupload
             name="files[]"
```

```
                    data-url="/server/uploadFile"
                    multiple
                    done="uploadFinished(e, data)">
    </body>

    </html>
```

Our input tag just has the following additions:

fileupload

> This marks the input tag as a file upload element.

data-url

> This is used by the FileUpload plug-in to decide where to upload the file to. In our
> example, we assume there is a server API waiting at */server/uploadFile* to process
> the data it sends.

multiple

> The multiple attribute tells the directive (and the fileupload widget) to allow it
> to select multiple files at once. We get this for free from the plug-in without needing
> to write a single additional line of code. Again, this is a built-in plug-in bonus.

done

> This is the AngularJS function to call when the plug-in finishes uploading the se-
> lected file. We could add similar ones for progress if we wanted to. This also speci-
> fies the two arguments that our directive calls.

So what does the controller backing this look like? Pretty much what you would expect
it to look like:

```
var app = angular.module('myApp', ['myApp.directives']);

app.controller('MainCtrl', function($scope) {
  $scope.uploadFinished = function(e, data) {
    console.log('We just finished uploading this baby...');
  };
});
```

And with that, we have a simple, working, reusable file upload directive.

Using Socket.IO

A common requirement for the web nowadays is real-time web applications, which
need to be updated as soon as the data on the server is updated. Previously used techniques such as polling have been found lacking, and sometimes we just want to open a
socket to our client and communicate.

Socket.IO (*http://socket.io/*) is a brilliant library that allows you to do just that, and uses
a dead simple, event-based API to allow you to develop real-time web apps. We are going

---

to develop a real-time, anonymous broadcast system (think Twitter, without usernames) that allows users to broadcast a message to all Socket.IO's users and see all the messages. Nothing will be stored, so all messages will only be alive for as long as a given user is active, but that will be sufficient to demonstrate how nicely Socket.IO can integrate into AngularJS.

Right off, we are going to wrap Socket.IO into a nice AngularJS service. By doing so, we can ensure that:

- Socket.IO events are noticed and handled within the AngularJS lifecycle
- It becomes easy to test the integration later

```
var app = angular.module('myApp', []);

// We define the socket service as a factory so that it
// is instantiated only once, and thus acts as a singleton
// for the scope of the application.
app.factory('socket', function ($rootScope) {
  var socket = io.connect('http://localhost:8080');
  return {
    on: function (eventName, callback) {
      socket.on(eventName, function () {
        var args = arguments;
        $rootScope.$apply(function () {
          callback.apply(socket, args);
        });
      });
    },
    emit: function (eventName, data, callback) {
      socket.emit(eventName, data, function () {
        var args = arguments;
        $rootScope.$apply(function () {
          if (callback) {
            callback.apply(socket, args);
          }
        });
      })
    }
  };
});
```

We are just wrapping the two functions we care about, which are the on event and broadcast event methods of the Socket.IO API. There are a bunch more, and they can be wrapped in a similar manner.

We are going to have a simple *index.html*, which shows a textbox with a send button and a list of messages. In this example, we do not keep track of who sends the messages or when they are sent.

```
<!DOCTYPE html>
<html ng-app="myApp">

<head lang="en">
  <meta charset="utf-8">
  <title>Anonymous Broadcaster</title>
  <script src="/socket.io/socket.io.js">
  </script>
  <script
    src="http://ajax.googleapis.com/ajax/libs/angularjs/1.0.3/angular.min.js">
  </script>

  <script src="app.js"></script>
</head>
<body ng-controller="MainCtrl">
    <input type="text" ng-model="message">
    <button ng-click="broadcast()">Broadcast</button>

    <ul>
      <li ng-repeat="msg in messages">{{msg}}</li>
    </ul>
</body>
</html>
```

Let's go to our `MainCtrl` (this is part of *app.js*), which is where we pull this all together:

```
function MainCtrl($scope, socket) {

  $scope.message = '';
  $scope.messages = [];

  // When we see a new msg event from the server
  socket.on('new:msg', function (message) {
    $scope.messages.push(message);
  });

  // Tell the server there is a new message
  $scope.broadcast = function() {
    socket.emit('broadcast:msg', {message: $scope.message});
    $scope.messages.push($scope.message);
    $scope.message = '';
  };
}
```

The controller itself is quite simple. It listens for events on the socket connection, and whenever the user presses the broadcast button, lets the server know that there is a new message. It also adds it to the message list to display immediately to the user.

Then we have the final piece, the server. This is a NodeJS server that knows how to serve the app code, and also simultaneously create a Socket.IO server.

```
var app = require('express')()
  , server = require('http').createServer(app)
```

```
  , io = require('socket.io').listen(server);

server.listen(8080);

app.get('/', function (req, res) {
  res.sendfile(__dirname + '/index.html');
});

app.get('/app.js', function(req, res) {
  res.sendfile(__dirname + '/app.js');
});

io.sockets.on('connection', function (socket) {
  socket.emit('new:msg', 'Welcome to AnonBoard');

  socket.on('broadcast:msg', function(data) {
    // Tell all the other clients (except self) about the new message
    socket.broadcast.emit('new:msg', data.message);
  });
});
```

You could easily expand this later to handle more messages and more intricate structures, but this example lays the foundation on which you can implement socket con-
nections between your client and server.

The app is very simple. It does not do any validation (whether the messages are empty),
but it does have the HTML sanitization that AngularJS provides by default. It does not
handle complex messages, but it does offer a fully working end-to-end Socket.IO implementation integrated into AngularJS that you can now build your work off of.

A Simple Pagination Service

A very common use case for most web apps is to display a list of items. More often than
not, we have more data than can be reasonably displayed on a single page. In such a
case, we want to display the data in a paginated manner, with an ability to move to the
next and previous pages. Since this is a common requirement throughout the app, it
makes sense to extract this functionality into a common, reusable Paginator service.

Our Paginator service (a very simple implementation) is going to allow users of the
service to tell the service how to fetch the data, given an offset and limit, as well as the
page size. It will internally handle all the logic of figuring out which items to fetch, which
page is next, whether there is a next page, and so on.

This service could be extended further to cache items within the service, but that is left
as an exercise for the user. All our example will entail is storing the currentPageI
tems field in a cache, retrieving it from there if it is available, and going to the fetch
Function otherwise.

Let's take a look at the service implementation:

```
angular.module('services', []).factory('Paginator', function() {
  // Despite being a factory, the user of the service gets a new
  // Paginator every time he calls the service. This is because
  // we return a function that provides an object when executed

  return function(fetchFunction, pageSize) {
    var paginator = {
      hasNextVar: false,
      next: function() {
        if (this.hasNextVar) {
          this.currentOffset += pageSize;
          this._load();
        }
      },
      _load: function() {
        var self = this;
        fetchFunction(this.currentOffset, pageSize + 1, function(items) {
          self.currentPageItems = items.slice(0, pageSize);
          self.hasNextVar = items.length === pageSize + 1;
        });
      },
      hasNext: function() {
        return this.hasNextVar;
      },
      previous: function() {
        if(this.hasPrevious()) {
          this.currentOffset -= pageSize;
          this._load();
        }
      },
      hasPrevious: function() {
        return this.currentOffset !== 0;
      },
      currentPageItems: [],
      currentOffset: 0
    };

    // Load the first page
    paginator._load();
    return paginator;
  };
});
```

The Paginator service expects two arguments when it is called: a fetch function, and the size of each page. The fetch function expects the following signature:

```
fetchFunction(offset, limit, callback);
```

It will then be called with the correct offset and limit by the Paginator whenever it needs to fetch and display a certain page. Internal to the function, it can either slice the data from a large array, or go to the server and make a call to fetch the data. When the data is available, the fetch function needs to call the callback function with it.

Let us take a look at the spec for this, to clarify how we could use it when we have a large array with too many items returned to us. Note that this is a unit test. Because of the way it is implemented, we can test the service independent of any controller or XHR requests.

```
describe('Paginator Service', function() {

    beforeEach(module('services'));

    var paginator;

    var items = [1, 2, 3, 4, 5, 6];
    var fetchFn = function(offset, limit, callback) {
      callback(items.slice(offset, offset + limit));
    };

    beforeEach(inject(function(Paginator) {
      paginator = Paginator(fetchFn, 3);
    }));

    it('should show items on the first page', function() {
      expect(paginator.currentPageItems).toEqual([1, 2, 3]);
      expect(paginator.hasNext()).toBeTruthy();
      expect(paginator.hasPrevious()).toBeFalsy();
    });

    it('should go to the next page', function() {
      paginator.next();
      expect(paginator.currentPageItems).toEqual([4, 5, 6]);
      expect(paginator.hasNext()).toBeFalsy();
      expect(paginator.hasPrevious()).toBeTruthy();
    });

    it('should go to previous page', function() {
      paginator.next();
      expect(paginator.currentPageItems).toEqual([4, 5, 6]);
      paginator.previous();
      expect(paginator.currentPageItems).toEqual([1, 2, 3]);
    });

    it('should not go next from last page', function() {
      paginator.next();
      expect(paginator.currentPageItems).toEqual([4, 5, 6]);
      paginator.next();
      expect(paginator.currentPageItems).toEqual([4, 5, 6]);
    });

    it('should not go back from first page', function() {
      paginator.previous();
```

```
      expect(paginator.currentPageItems).toEqual([1, 2, 3]);
    });
  });
```

The Paginator exposes `currentPageItems` on itself, which can then be bound from the templates on a `repeater` (or however else you want to display them). The `hasNext()` and `hasPrevious()` can be used to figure out when to show the Next and Previous Page links, and on `click`, it just needs to call `next()` or `previous()`, respectively.

How would you use this with something that needs to fetch data from the server for each page? Here is what a possible controller that fetches search results from the server one page at a time could look like:

```
var app = angular.module('myApp', ['myApp.services']);

app.controller('MainCtrl', ['$scope', '$http', 'Paginator',
  function($scope, $http, Paginator) {
    $scope.query = 'Testing';
    var fetchFunction = function(offset, limit, callback) {
      $http.get('/search',
          {params: {query: $scope.query, offset: offset, limit: limit}})
          .success(callback);
    };

    $scope.searchPaginator = Paginator(fetchFunction, 10);
}]);
```

The HTML page could use the Pagination service as follows:

```
<!DOCTYPE html>
<html ng-app="myApp">

<head lang="en">
  <meta charset="utf-8">
  <title>Pagination Service</title>

  <script
      src="http://ajax.googleapis.com/ajax/libs/angularjs/1.0.3/angular.min.js">
  </script>
  <script src="pagination.js"></script>
  <script src="app.js"></script>
</head>

<body ng-controller="MainCtrl">
  <input type="text" ng-model="query">
  <ul>
    <li ng-repeat="item in searchPaginator.currentPageItems">
      {{item}}
    </li>
  </ul>
  <a href=""
      ng-click="searchPaginator.previous()"
```

```
            ng-show="searchPaginator.hasPrevious()">&lt;&lt; Prev</a>
    <a href=""
            ng-click="searchPaginator.next()"
            ng-show="searchPaginator.hasNext()">Next &gt;&gt;</a>
</body>

</html>
```

Working with Servers and Login

One final example will actually cover a multitude of scenarios, most or all of them linked with the $http resource. In our experience, the $http service is one of the core services in AngularJS. But it can be extended to do a lot of the common requirements of a web app, including:

- Having a common error-handling point
- Handling authorization and login redirects
- Working with servers that don't understand or speak JSON
- Talking with external services (outside the same origin) via JSONP

So in this (slightly contrived) example, we will have the skeleton of a full-fledged app that will:

1. Show all unrecoverable errors (Non 401s) in a `butterbar` directive that gets shown on all screens only when an error exists.
2. Have an `ErrorService` which will be used for communicating between the directive, the view, and the controllers.
3. Fire an event (`event:loginRequired`) whenever the server responds with a 401. This will then get handled by a root controller that oversees the entire application.
4. Handle requests that need to be made to the server with some authorization headers that are specific to the current user.

We will not go over the entire application (the routes, the templates, and so on), as most of those are fairly straightforward. We will highlight only the pieces that are relevant (so you can copy and paste that into your codebase and get started right away). These will be fully functional. If you want to revisit defining Services and Factories, jump to Chapter 7. If you want to take a look at how to work with servers, you can refer to Chapter 5.

Let us first take a look at the Error service:

```
var servicesModule = angular.module('myApp.services', []);

servicesModule.factory('errorService', function() {
```

```
    return {
      errorMessage: null,
      setError: function(msg) {
        this.errorMessage = msg;
      },
      clear: function() {
        this.errorMessage = null;
      }
    };
  });
```

Our error message directive, which is actually independent of the Error service, would just look for an alert message attribute, and then bind to it. It would conditionally show itself when the alert message is present.

```
// USAGE: <div alert-bar alertMessage="myMessageVar"></div>
angular.module('myApp.directives', []).
  directive('alertBar', ['$parse', function($parse) {
    return {
      restrict: 'A',
      template: '<div class="alert alert-error alert-bar"' +
        'ng-show="errorMessage">' +
        '<button type="button" class="close" ng-click="hideAlert()">' +
        'x</button>' +
        '{{errorMessage}}</div>',

      link: function(scope, elem, attrs) {
        var alertMessageAttr = attrs['alertmessage'];
        scope.errorMessage = null;

        scope.$watch(alertMessageAttr, function(newVal) {
          scope.errorMessage = newVal;
        });
        scope.hideAlert = function() {
          scope.errorMessage = null;
          // Also clear the error message on the bound variable.
          // Do this so that if the same error happens again
          // the alert bar will be shown again next time.
          $parse(alertMessageAttr).assign(scope, null);
        };
      }
    };
  }]);
```

We would then add the alert bar to the HTML as follows:

```
<div alert-bar alertmessage="errorService.errorMessage"></div>
```

We need to ensure that the ErrorService is saved on the scope of the controller as "errorService" before we add the preceding HTML. That is, if RootController was the controller responsible for having the AlertBar, then:

```
app.controller('RootController',
               ['$scope', 'ErrorService', function($scope, ErrorService) {
  $scope.errorService = ErrorService;
});
```

That gives us a decent framework to show and hide errors and alerts. Now let us see how we can tackle the various status codes that the server can throw at us, through the use of an interceptor:

```
servicesModule.config(function ($httpProvider) {
  $httpProvider.responseInterceptors.push('errorHttpInterceptor');
});

// register the interceptor as a service
// intercepts ALL angular ajax HTTP calls
servicesModule.factory('errorHttpInterceptor',
    function ($q, $location, ErrorService, $rootScope) {
  return function (promise) {
    return promise.then(function (response) {
      return response;
    }, function (response) {
      if (response.status === 401) {
        $rootScope.$broadcast('event:loginRequired');
      } else if (response.status >= 400 && response.status < 500) {
        ErrorService.setError('Server was unable to find' +
          ' what you were looking for... Sorry!!');
      }
      return $q.reject(response);
    });
  };
});
```

Now all that needs to happen is for some controller somewhere to listen for a loginRequired event, and redirect to the login page (or do something more complex, like display a modal dialog with login options).

```
$scope.$on('event:loginRequired', function() {
  $location.path('/login');
});
```

That just leaves requests that will need authorization. Let us just say that all requests that require authorization will need a header—"Authorization"—which will have a value that is specific for the current user that is logged in. Since this will change every time, we cannot use default transformRequests, as those are config level changes. We will instead wrap the $http service, and create our own AuthHttp service.

We will also have an Authentication service that is responsible for storing the user's auth information (fetched however you want, normally as part of the login process). The AuthHttp service will refer to this Authentication service and add the necessary headers to authorize the requests.

```
// This factory is only evaluated once, and authHttp is memorized. That is,
// future requests to authHttp service return the same instance of authHttp
servicesModule.factory('authHttp', function($http, Authentication) {
  var authHttp = {};

  // Append the right header to the request
  var extendHeaders = function(config) {
    config.headers = config.headers || {};
    config.headers['Authorization'] = Authentication.getTokenType() +
        ' ' + Authentication.getAccessToken();
  };

  // Do this for each $http call
  angular.forEach(['get', 'delete', 'head', 'jsonp'], function(name) {
    authHttp[name] = function(url, config) {
      config = config || {};
      extendHeaders(config);
      return $http[name](url, config);
    };
  });

  angular.forEach(['post', 'put'], function(name) {
    authHttp[name] = function(url, data, config) {
      config = config || {};
      extendHeaders(config);
      return $http[name](url, data, config);
    };
  });

  return authHttp;
});
```

Any request that requires authorization will be made via authHttp.get() instead of $http.get(). As long as the Authentication service is set with the right information, your calls will fly through with ease. We use a service for Authentication as well, so that the information is available throughout the app, without having to refetch it every time the route changes.

That pretty much covers all the pieces we would need for this application. You should be able to just copy the code right out of here, paste into your application, and make it work for you. Good luck!

Conclusion

While this brings us to the end of our book, we are nowhere near close to covering everything about AngularJS. Our aim with this book was to provide a solid foundation from which one can begin her explorations and become comfortable with developing in AngularJS. To this extent, we covered all the basics (and some advanced topics), while providing as many examples as we could along the way.

Are we done? No. There is still a great amount to learn about how AngularJS operates under the covers. We didn't touch upon creating complex, interdependent directives, for example. There is so much more out there, that three or even four books wouldn't be enough. But we hope that this book gives you the confidence to be able to tackle much more complex requirements head on.

We had a great time writing this book, and hope to see some amazing applications written in AngularJS out on the Internet.

Index

We'd like to hear your suggestions for improving our indexes. Send email to index@oreilly.com.

HTML validation, 119
HTML5, 43, 119, 138, 140
HTML5 cookies, 148
HTTP headers, setting, 104
HTTP protocol, 42

I

i18n/L10n, 149
IDs, 2, 19, 125
IE (Internet Explorer), 81, 122
if-else operator, 27
image tags, 26
index.html, 149
indices, 22
initialization process, 126
inline event handlers, 19
inline styles, 24
input, validation of, 45, 94
integration tests, 49, 56
internationalization, 148
isDisabled property, 24
isolate scopes, 128
item property, in shopping cart example, 7

J

Jasmine tests, 49, 54, 96
Java, 12
JavaScript
    eval() function, 27
    main method, 142
    writing unobtrusive, 19
jqLite wrapper, 132
jQuery, 4, 102, 132
jQuery Datepickers, 153–157
JS library dependencies, 48
JS source files, 48
JSON, 171
JSON vulnerability, 116
JSONP, 42, 171
JSP, 3

K

Karma, 52, 55, 56, 71
keyboard focus, 43

L

Law of Demeter, 5

library, loading of, 11
link href values, 90
link property, 120, 126
links
    emailing, 41
    relative links, 142
    rewriting, 142
linky filter, 152
List Controller, 86, 91, 97
lists, 21, 157
loading, 143
localization, 148
logic
    avoiding in templates, 26, 79
    business logic, 78
login errors, 171
looping constructs, 27

M

main method, 142
malicious sites, 116
mandatory fields, 45
manual testing, 57
mathematics functions, 27
menus, conditional disabling of, 24
method calls, 102
minification, 57, 66
minimum/maximum field lengths, 95
mobile apps, 41, 58
mock data, 34
model data
    observing changes with, 29
    publishing with scopes, 28, 128–131
    storage of, 3
model objects, creating, 13, 108
model properties, binding elements to, 16
model variables, 12
Model View Controller (MVC)
    basics of, 3, 12
models
    as basis for apps, 79
    basics of, 12, 78
    model trees in Batarang, 60
module class, 144
modules
    creation of, 14
    module methods, 142–146
    number needed, 36
    organization of, 143

About the Authors

Brad Green works at Google as an engineering manager. In addition to the AngularJS project, Brad also directs Accessibility and Support Engineering. Prior to Google, Brad worked on the early mobile web at AvantGo, founded and sold startups, and spent a few hard years toiling as a caterer. Brad's first job out of school was as a lackey to Steve Jobs at NeXT Computer, writing demo software and designing Jobs' slide presentations. Brad lives in Mountain View, CA, with his wife and two children.

Shyam Seshadri is the owner and CEO of Fundoo Solutions (*http://www.befun doo.com*), where he splits his time between working on innovative and exciting new products for the Indian market, and consulting about and running workshops on AngularJS. Prior to Fundoo Solutions, Shyam completed his MBA from the prestigious Indian School of Business in Hyderabad. Shyam's first job out of college was with Google, where he worked on multiple projects, including Google Feedback (AngularJS's first customer!), and various internal tools and projects. Shyam currently operates from his office in Navi Mumbai, India.

Colophon

The animal on the cover of *AngularJS* is a thornback cowfish (*Ostraciidae*). This fish of many names—thornback, thornback cow, backspine cowfish, shortspined cowfish, blue-spotted cowfish—is usually found on rocky reefs or sandy slopes in a tangle of sponge and weeds in the Western Indo-Pacific region. They feed primarily on worms and other invertebrates.

These boxfish can grow up to 15 centimeters long and anywhere between 3 to 50 meters wide. Members of the boxfish family are recognizable by the hexagonal pattern on their skin. Their bodies are shaped like a boxy triangle from which their fins, tail, eyes, and mouth protrude, allowing them to swim with a rowing motion. As they age, their shapes change from more rounded to more square-shaped, and their brighter colors dim.

The thornback cowfish protects itself by secreting cationic surfactants through their skin, which is triggered by stress. The toxins, usually secreted in the form of a mucus, dissolve into the environment and irritate fish in the surrounding area.

The cover image is from *Johnson's Natural History*. The cover font is Adobe ITC Garamond. The text font is Adobe Minion Pro; the heading font is Adobe Myriad Condensed; and the code font is Dalton Maag's Ubuntu Mono.

Have it your way.